Dawn French, Jennifer Saunders and Ruby Wax wish to thank:

Joan Greenwood
Trevor Leighton (photographer extraordinaire)
Naomi Donne (Mrs Make-up)
Ben Elton
Ivor Sexton
Ian McKellen
Simon Brint
Roland Rivron
Fatima Namdar
Lesley Schiff
Sue Thompson
Frances Haggett
Sheila Colline
Nick Sayers
Steve Savage
Ros Saunders

Paul Jackson
Trevor Walton
All at Witzend

Ibiza
Crochetta

Ruby Wax would like to personally thank her dermatologist, her therapist, her orthodontist, her cosmetic surgeon, her hairdresser, for making her presence possible.

DAWN FRENCH   RUBY WAX   JENNIFER SAUNDERS

GiRLS on TOP

GRAFTON BOOKS
A Division of the Collins Publishing Group

LONDON GLASGOW
TORONTO SYDNEY AUCKLAND

Grafton Books
A Division of the Collins Publishing Group
8 Grafton Street, London W1X 3LA

A Grafton Paperback Original 1986

ISBN 0-586-06892-9

Printed in Great Britain by
St Edmundsbury Press Ltd, Bury St Edmunds, Suffolk

The publishers acknowledge the permission of Central
Independent Television plc to use the photographs on
pages   ii, 33 (Ali McGraw), 92 and 93 (Lady Carlton),
102, 112; the photographs on pages ii, 33, 92 and 93, 102, 121
copyright © 1985 Central Independent Television plc.

All other photographs by Trevor Leighton

Designed by Ros Saunders
Illustrations by Ivor Sexton

FOREWORD

BY BEN ELTON

Welcome to the *Girls on Top* book, unless you happen to be a browser in a book shop with no cash, in which case naff off and stop bending the pages.

Anyway, about the book. I think a book is bound to be good value when even the title is a gag, especially a rudie one and I don't think I'm giving anything away when I reveal that the phrase 'Girls on Top' not only means sisters being strong and successful despite a sexist society, but it also means bonking in a really great way. Clever stuff, eh? I didn't get it for ages.

Incidentally, the fact that this book has been written by women does not mean that men cannot buy it: where cash is concerned these girlies don't give a toss about politics. (You notice I say 'girlies' there: I do this because 'stupid bloody no-nobs' might be considered a bit sexist).

Anyway, the one thing that must be got absolutely straight right now is that this is *not* a spin-off. So many books are written to cash in on a TV series ('Oliver Twist' 'Tender is the Night' 'The Blue Peter Annual') that the stupid bloody no-nobs asked me to make it quite clear that this is not that type of book, this is an even crappier type of book. Because it is not written by those tossy girls at all, it is written by a lesbian computer called Greta. The fact that Greta chose to use the same names and everything as in the TV series is an unfortunate coincidence. No way is this a spin-off.

So here we are then, this is it, and what am I doing in it? Well basically, Dawn, Jennifer and Ruby promised that if I did the intro, I could have some serious, bitch action sex stuff with the authors, trousers down and *everything*. Well of course being blind and stupid I agreed. It was only afterwards that they told me about Greta saying that if I wanted to put my nob in a computer, fine, but it seemed a bit pervy to them and they'd have to call the police. So I ended up having to write the intro for nothing, no sex and no cash. I'm not so much bitter, as incredibly pissed off. Incidentally the reason for having an intro is so an independent witness can say how great the main act is, well they're not, they're crap, and so's their book and so's their series and I really really mean that, it's not just a groovy joke amongst mates, it really really is crap. Enjoy it.

BEN ELTON
(Feminist author and great bonk)

WHOSE LIVES ARE ENDANGERED ANYWAY?

Here's me doing my pro-fur speech, showing skins to the poor ↓

THE PRO - FUR ARGUMENT.

SPEECH BY SHELLEY DUPONT TO BE DELIVERED AT HYDE PARK ...

WHEN THE SUN'S OUT   (TAN WEATHER)

1.   I'm standing on this box today because me and my full-
     length chinchilla have been smirked at once too often
     by people who obviously can't afford to buy a fur coat.
     I say throw a tuft of lynx on them and they'll be
     blowing a different tune.   In this speech whenever
     LEAVE TIME FOR APPLAUSE
                    I refer to "they" or "them", I will be
                         refering to those anti-fur fanatics which
                              include lesbians, poor people, social workers and
                              all others who refuse to shave under their pits or
                              wash their hair.

← *This is the type I mean*

          2.   First and foremost important in the "why animals should be
     fur coats" argument is that I look fabulous in fur. Be it from mink to any
     old dog I may have run over in my BMW.   **LEAVE TIME FOR APPLAUSE**
     The feeling of dead carcass near to my flesh just makes me glow all over.
     Backing me up on this fact is my mother and anyone from my neighborhood in
     Beverly Hills.

3.   My next fact is that the very animals "they" (poor people etc.) are so
     enamoured of, wear it, and if it's good enough for something that crawls on
     all fours and licks itself, it is certainly good enough for Shelley Dupont.
     → You! Do you think it's fair some otter who sleeps in twigs should be
Direct this question to someone in a cloth coat

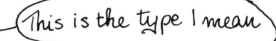

allowed to wear fifteen thousand dollars worth of pelt on its back? Do you????!!!! You in the really flattering third-world-combat-sack-that-I-wouldn't-wrap-a-corpse-in? I mean what have animals ever done besides dig holes and shed. It's not like skinning Glenda Jackson and wearing her stole. I'm wearing something that pees on grass. And if you love these animals so much, why haven't I ever met anyone with a racoon or a cheetah as a house-pet? You love them in the jungle, but not in your own home. Who's a racist now?   the one smirking now ... yes.

If there's a heckler I can say: "Hey, pox-face, the closest you've come to a mink is being bitten by one" That should shut him up.

Leave time for guilt to sink in.

THE HAPPY FOX FUR

4.   And I personally think I'm giving most animals something they could never experience in "nature". I'm wearing them into some of the best restaurants in Europe. I mean one day they're hunting worms, the next day they're having tea at the Ritz. And all I ask of them is to go to the dry-cleaners twice a year. What a life!!

To another heckler, if there is one: "O.K thunder-thighs, you tell me how many foxes you've seen go into Saks Fifth Avenue"

5.   Plus all this crap about being endangered. Well, whose fault is that? they have legs: they should run away if there's a problem. I mean if they're stupid enough to just stand there while someone shoots at them, then they deserve to have buttons sewn on them. *To heckler: "Up yours"*

6. Also a word about animals who may be going extinct. Well, I can't think of a better way to become immortal than a Pierre Cardin label on your neck. You may not be scampering through a field, but at least people will remember what you looked like, which is important if you're the last one left in a species.

7. Well, that about covers my argument for why animals should die. If God didn't want to see them in shops, he would have given them hand-guns, right? They already make great glue, steak and moisturizer ... I mean they're dead anyway, so why should we throw away thousands of dollars worth of peel? In conclusion, as long as there's a fox, racoon or mink roaming around happy and free and within target range, this gal will be wearin' a fur. Thank you.

LET APPLAUSE RUN RAMPANT.
~~~~~~~~~~~~~~~~~~~~~~~~~~~
Hand-out swatches of fur
to poor people so they know
what they're missing.

Candy... "How I called it Quits with Curtis"

by Gabby Fontayne

SHE IS GIRLISH, GORGEOUS AND GIGGLY. At one glance her doe eyes seem to say, 'Spank me, I'm naughty', yet at another they say, 'Love me, I'm a woman'. She's strawberry blonde and vivacious, with a tinkling Minnie Mouse laugh hiding the razor-sharp cunning that's put her where she is today . . . a second floor flat in trendy Chelsea.

VITAL STATISTICS
Candice Valentine, 21 . . . (other vital statistics include 36″, 24″, 6½″, but she teasingly won't divulge what belongs where), is a model whose pictures have been seen on locker doors and garage walls all over the country. She purrs, 'It's incredible, because d'you know, I can't even drive.'

ON THE CHAISE LONGUE
As Candy and I sipped crème de menthe and coke together on an antique victorian chaise longue, the door burst open and in came three strange girls. 'Flatmates?' I asked. After she quickly ushered them out, a flicker of concern crossed her kittenish face. She whispered, 'Well, Jennifer is mentally disabled, Amanda is a Vietnam war veteran, and Shelley, well,

she's got this disease where she thinks everyone else is deaf . . . so you see, they're all social outcasts – I can't cure them, but I can and will give them a home . . . and love.' And so she revealed that she supports all three girls on her meagre model's salary.

I could have listened to her talk all day long about how many other disabled, 'helpless' friends she supports, but I knew that wasn't the story she had called me up to talk about. I sensed troubled waters, so I quickly got to business and asked her the wheres, hows and whos of her relationship with that saucy, dashing, Bronx-talking boy-next-door from 'Spartacus', TONY CURTIS.

HOT
I asked whether it was true that 'Some Like It Hot?'. Choking back the emotion, she said, 'I first met him by chance at a charity celebrity disco-dancerama for the blind, deaf and mute bubble-children fundraiser that I helped to organize. I was dancing with something in calipers that would break your heart, when Tony interrupted and said in his native Bronx, 'Can I have this dance, doll?'. I closed my eyes and held my arms out. This was my matinée idol . . . eventually I opened my eyes and saw Tony waltzing off with the caliper girl.

LOVE AT FIRST SIGHT
'At that very moment I knew I was a teeny bit in love,' she said, in a hushed voice, hardly audible.

TELEPHONE RINGING
She arrived home that night to a ringing telephone only to pick it up and hear the raspy Bronx twang of 'My love-torn Tony'.

DRUNKEN STUPOR

He explained that he had been helplessly drunk and had been the unfortunate victim of double vision. He begged her forgiveness and they made plans for a secret date. From that date on, it was a whirlwind of tête-à-tête lunches, cuddles in Covent Garden and moonlit frolickings in Wapping (Candice's home).

BOOBS

'I made a lot of boobs when I first introduced him to my mum, but she thought he was a lovely bloke anyway, even with the toupee.'

HER PUD IN HIS MOUTH

'It was so funny one Sunday lunch . . . she gave him four Yorkshire Puds and said, "You need a bit of fattening up, give our Cand something to hold on to." He put my hand in his lap and said, "She's got all she can hold on to here." Well!!! Excuse me!! Laugh? We were nearly sick!' She chuckled at the memory.

'Anyway, seriously, although our love was growing at an enormous rate, we never "touched", because both of us felt it would "soil" our lovely relationship. We talked a lot about, oh y'know, does God exist, capital punishment, tooth decay, that sort of thing.'

It all seemed like a dream until Tony got 'that' call from California which they had been dreading.

24 HOURS

'He looked me in the eye and said "I'll give you 24 hours to decide if you want to give up your career and come to live with me in the fast lane of heady Beverly Hills' . . . That was the worst night of torment for me, ever. I missed Dallas and chewed off two of my best nails trying to decide.' Candice sobbed, clutched a tissue during this part of her

story, and pleaded with me to turn off my mini-tape recorder . . . I did, and she continued:

'I rang him and said 'Tone, I said, I have nearly got a career as a successful model, life is more than sex-orgies and beach barbecues in Malibu, and ending up being known to everyone as just plain old "Mrs Curtis".' . . . He was silent then, and I knew that he understood . . .'

BLUE

These two love-birds haven't spoken since that day, but their hearts are united somewhere over the blue, blue Atlantic Ocean.

'I'll never forget him,' she sobbed. I asked her what she was going to do with the £20,000 she got for this exclusive story . . . She told me that she was going to set up a fund to support other women involved with famous Hollywood stars, called 'The Hollywood Heartbreakers' fund.

A heart of gold and hair to match. Candice's Valentine won't be coming from California this year.

(Next week's exclusive with Candice . . . 'So you think Paul Newman's happily married?')

Raise both arms over head . . . feel it burn. Cross legs, feet on floor . . . come on and get sweaty!
Hold that position . . . owwwww: ladies get into the groove! Flick left wrist and place right hand on hip
. . . let scarf dangle . . . I'm feeling good now. Put left leg forward on floor. Now you're really moving.
Hunch left shoulder, curl fingers, bend legs . . . get down and work it . . . let those knees crunch.

THE LADY CARLTON WORK-OUT

Nature has blessed me from birth with an over-abundance of grace.
What better way can I repay her than by transforming myself into the oracle of beauty itself?
Below are my exercises for physical perfection.
Perform them daily and witness your own heavenly transformation.

Crunching's only your cramping joints saying 'Thank you.' Heart should be pounding wildly, pulse racing, muscle spasms, . . . hands on floor, buttock arisen, breakfast's coming up . . . go with it. Whiplash backwards, feel that head crack, slip that disc, collapse completely, blood pressure soaring, check heartbeat, (IF ANY) and say, 'Thank you body, let's have a large gin . . . cheers.'

A freeform
'DANCE
OF THE
MUSE'

–Inspiration

SPARE *Cheeks*

▶ **AMANDA RIPLEY'S GUIDE TO peace camp fashion**

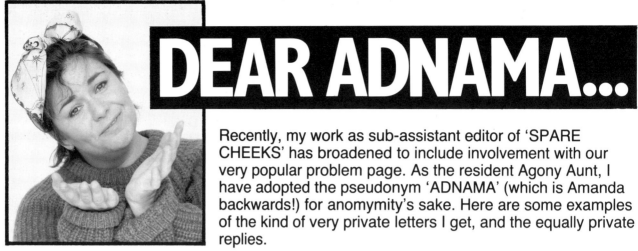

DEAR ADNAMA...

Recently, my work as sub-assistant editor of 'SPARE CHEEKS' has broadened to include involvement with our very popular problem page. As the resident Agony Aunt, I have adopted the pseudonym 'ADNAMA' (which is Amanda backwards!) for anomymity's sake. Here are some examples of the kind of very private letters I get, and the equally private replies.

Dear Adnama,
My husband has recently developed a serious blood disease and gone into hospital. He has consequently lost his job and I'm finding it very hard to cope both financially and mentally ... what should I do?
Worried, Hants.

Dear Mrs Worried over nothing,
Well, let's face facts and admit that it's pretty obvious that he's going to die, so my advice is this ...
Leave home now, whilst he's safely tucked away in the sick bin. Make sure that your insurance policy is up to date with the payments, thereby avoiding any unpleasant funeral costs. Come on, pull yourself together gal, come and live in London. There are so many people in this metropolis, I'm sure someone will put you up. If not, there's always a bed at the Christian Sappho Hospice in Soho. You may well bump into me personally, I'm forever there doing good work. Also get in touch with Hildegarde on 01-600 7910, because she's got lots of work (voluntary flag selling in aid of the politically dead, for instance) to tide you over, O.K.?
Courage mon brave comrade,
Love, A♀

Dear Adnama,
I have recently got married and I am trying to help my husband come to terms with my feminist principles ... is it right for instance, that I should always wash up?
Yours in bondage,
Mrs Mapin

Dear Mrs married to a bastard,
Ask yourself, is it right that Chile always had to get trampled on? Or is it right that Vietnam was considered to be a buffer state? And what about Sweden? If you know the answers to these questions (and I think you do) never wash up again.
If you want to live your whole life in total torture, go ahead, stay married.
Yours, with love,
A♀

Dear Adnama,
I read your letters each week, and I think you're great.
Love,
Karen

My dear Karen,
Wanna collect a signed photograph in person?
53, Oak Park Gardens, Chelsea ... ANYTIME.
Lovesya,
Mandy ♀♡

Dear Adnama,
Is your name really Amanda Ripley, and are you that bossy little do-gooder who charged me to come to a meeting about Women in Electricity?
If so I'd like to ram a marrow ...

A QUICKIE

SPOT THE BALL

An in-depth interview with Shelley Dupont . . . by Shelley Dupont

I met Ms Dupont at Brown's Hotel in fashionable London W1 for tea. Shelley looked incredible . . . she just exudes inherited wealth. She entered in a blaze of fuchsia and bronze waving to everyone in sight. Some waved back. Shelley demanded her usual table, then noticed some tourists (Shelley pronounced this word with a disapproving hissing sound) were sitting there. At a snap of her fingers, Lorenzo the *maître d'* had them removed. Shelley ordered a

My first part was playing a tin opener because I had a huge overbite. My mother realized she had a star as a child and bought me my own stage in our house. She'd invite all her friends over, lock all the doors and shout, 'Hit it, baby!' I'd pretend to be a fairy and just generally make magic, until everyone somehow managed to get out. (A lot of them used the windows till my mother had bars put up.) Then, years later I was accepted into the Bud Stanislovsky Academy,

face-to-face WITH A STAR

full cream tea and a burger with everything. I had the same. Heads turned and people pointed at Shelley recognizing the voice as she shouted not to 'burn the buns'. But Shelley gave them all the finger and they quickly turned away from her. I switched on my mini-tape recorder and began the interview with probably the biggest up-and-comer of the decade.

SHELLEY I'm telling you, these English . . . you make one perfectly normal request at a normal volume and they pucker their rectums.

SHELLEY OK Shelley, let's start: when did you first decide to go into show business?

SHELLEY Probably when I was still warm in the womb – no, seriously, I was about two years old and it was my birthday party. I remember I had pigged out on cake 'n' cookies and I threw up all over myself. Everyone just stopped and stared at me. I loved it and from that moment on I devoted my life to being the center of attention. I kept on throwing up on myself until, at eight, I discovered the stage.

Beverly Hills, which was brutal competition to get in (before you can get an audition your father has to be paying super-tax) and of course the rest is history.

SHELLEY Besides your stage work as a child, Shelley, what other experiences do you remember?

SHELLEY Well, I spent a lot of years at the 'Beverly Hills day camp for gorgeous children,' where we learnt how to be tough. I remember once they dropped us off on Rodeo Drive wearing no make-up in broad daylight to see how we'd survive.

SHELLEY My God, what did you do?

SHELLEY Well, Saks Fifth Avenue had a lot of samples in their cosmetics department.

SHELLEY What about your schooling? You went to Beverly Hills High – what did you study?

SHELLEY I majored in tipping and minored in tanning.

SHELLEY Any high school memories in particular?

SHELLEY There was a girl in my class from a minority. She was poor, and she couldn't afford a nose job like the rest of us, so as a favor I threw a basketball into her face, broke her nose and tried to sculpt it into a Aryan ski-jump-style nose like we were all wearing. Anyway I couldn't make it stand up: it kept collapsing into a snout shape – I was so embarrassed.

SHELLEY Oh, Shelley you're always thinking about other people aren't you. What are your politics?

SHELLEY My policy is that it's important to keep me rich, 'cause if I shopping, millions of people will become unemployed, not just in America, but all those Italian designers will suddenly find themselves in povertyville. But basically my political motto is based on nature: eat them before they eat you.

SHELLEY Any pet peeves?

SHELLEY Poor people who dress poor.

SHELLEY Have your parents helped you in any way?

SHELLEY Only financially. My father isn't at all interested in the arts and has only sneered at my success as a thespian. He's in sausages and I don't want to mention how many people who owed him money have ended up living in a salami. My mother is a professional out-patient, spending her time having parts of herself removed, lifted and shifted. What's originally left of her, I could carry in a hat box. And in those rare moments when she's unbandaged, she does volunteer work for 'Ax the blacks', 'Nix the spics' and 'Nuke the gooks' committees. Can I have some more food?

SHELLEY (To waiter) Another cream tea for Ms Dupont please. (To Shelley) Shelley where do you put it all?

SHELLEY Here. (Pointing to her svelte behind)

SHELLEY Oh Shelley, you have a gorgeous figure. You know a lot of women would like to look like you. What's your secret?

SHELLEY Well, basically my theory is to eat as much as you want as long as you make yourself throw up afterwards.

SHELLEY And how do you stay so young looking?

SHELLEY Fresh placenta. Never take frozen.

SHELLEY I could just go on talking to you forever, Shelley, but before we stop, any advice for other young hopefuls who want to make it like you did?

SHELLEY No.

SHELLEY Shelley was now busy eating her burger so I ended the interview. As she took an extra large bite, a dollop of ketchup ran down her front. I thought to myself, here sits a star in embryo with literally wall-to-wall talent and still she's so very, very human. She's just a great no matter how you slice her. ∎

AMANDA'S HOUSEHOLD TIPS

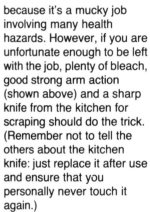

HOW TO CLEAN A TOILET

(and feel like you've done a real job)

Of course, prevention is better than cure. If only more people would just bother to swish the old brush around the bowl once a day, they wouldn't have the endless

problems that encrustment can bring . . . yellowish colouring, dirt rings and large insects floating around in the pan are the first giveaway signs of neglect. And before you know it, our old friend – unsightly deposits.

Come on now, we've all seen them and some people are more responsible for them than others, like Jennifer, for instance, who obviously doesn't know what a chain is for. The best way to deal with them is to get someone else to do it, because it's a mucky job involving many health hazards. However, if you are unfortunate enough to be left with the job, plenty of bleach, good strong arm action (shown above) and a sharp knife from the kitchen for scraping should do the trick. (Remember not to tell the others about the kitchen knife: just replace it after use and ensure that you personally never touch it again.)

Another easy solution is to buy one of those blue colouring tablets so that everyone is under the myth that nothing distasteful could possibly ever live in such a paradisial blue lagoon.

COLES THE PLUMBERS

WE PUT PIPES IN PLACES YOU NEVER THOUGHT YOU HAD

JULY 1986

1	Mon Jennifer's Xmas cake into oven.
2	Tue Make doyleys must buy glue.
3	Wed *AMANDA OVULATES. JENNIFER OUT OF HOSPITAL
4	Thur Candy to hospital for blood un-clotting
5	Fri Candy's mum goes into hospital (could die)
6	Sat Jennifer's Potential first period ever.
7	Sun Shelley - 1st silicone injection 1.45
8	Mon My little pony's tail and mane wash.
9	Tue Shet - phone Trevor Nunn - Again
10	Wed Shelley - find roots and re-tint
11	Thur Candy - charity disco-dancerama for kids
12	Fri Shelley - 2nd Silicone injection 3.30
13	Sat AMANDA'S WOMEN FOR POWER MEETING + SMEAR
14	Sun AMANDA'S WOMEN AGAINST POWER MEETING
15	Mon Candy to meet ATKWOOD - DORCHESTER. MOHAMMED - SAVOY
16	Tue AMANDA'S SLOOP INTERVIEW.! I W/A GIRL WHO ONCE KNEW SOMEONE WHO WORK'D W/A WOMAN WHO WAS NEIL KINNOCKS SEC. (ICHMED - SHERATON GOSSIPS W/ROD etc.

17	Wed Shelley - redo tummy tuck 10am.
18	Thur C - turned down marriage proposal from George Michael
19	Fri AMANDA'S POETRY NIGHT (THE WORKS OF VIRGINIA WADE
20	Sat Jennifer buys hampsters.
21	THIS MONTH'S SPARE - Candy major modelling SUN CHEEKS OUT assignment for titty-tales
22	Mon AMANDA'S MENSTRUATION TIME - Shelley moves into hotel.
23	Tue MUST FEED HAMPSTER - J
24	Wed Must feed hampster J.
25	Thur laundry day for Shelley (Jennifer scrub crotch (aways remember (pay you.)
26	Fri Must Buy flowers for hampsters grave.
27	Sat 3rd injection + Shelley's 1st bra - Ha-Hoo!!!
28	Sun JENNIFER'S XMAS CAKE OUT OF OVEN (AND INTO BIN (F I HAVE ANYTHING TO DO WITH IT!-A)
29	Mon Jennifer's resolution: must NOT EAT Christmas cake before Christmas.
30	Tue Shelley - major depilatory overhaul at Harveys hidden walls 2.00pm

Reminders

From Jennifer: Could someone please Return MY TERRAPIN?

MEMO FROM AMANDA - I FOUND SOMETHING AN ELEPHANT WOULD BE PROUD OF IN THE TOILET TODAY - PLEASE FLUSH IN FUTURE

MEMO TO JENNIFER - SOME FLAT OF OUR WILL SHELLEY'S - TAKE THE SMELL - I ONE SMELLING ONE HAIRS IN IT

♥ ♥ ♥ ♥ ♥ ♥ From Candy - Please don't drink my Perrier - its the only thing that keeps me alive ♥ ♥ ♥ ♥ ♥ ♥ ♥

Shelley - Can I borrow your earrings? Wonder No! item PleaSEE? Love Candy - Wonder No! item William

To EVERYONE Shelley Dupont has rented the Palladium on 22nd for a 'one-woman show. Give me the Claps. be there - or I'll never give you any money again

CHAPTER 8
Cosmetic Surgeons

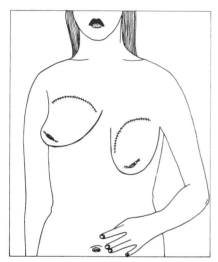

JUTMAN BREAST

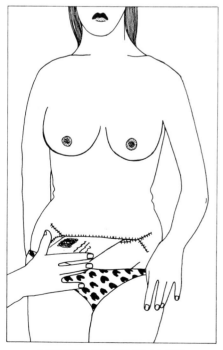

M^CMILLAN STOMACH

★★★★ Brilliant
★★★ Good
★ Start again
(no stars) Sue him

DR MICHAEL JUTMAN – *Breasts.* (no stars) First of all I hate his reception area. It's done in smoked glass and ultra suede with Dean Martin singing 'The Thrill of it All' over the speakers. There are a lot of 'Penthouses' thrown open with circles and arrows over the breasts and 'I did these' in Dr Jutman's handwriting.

You enter his office and either he's feeling you up or going straight to work, I can't tell which. He grabs your boobs and kneads them mumbling to himself 'Too pointy' or 'Come out, come out wherever you are' under his breath. He then snaps off the lights and flicks on a projection screen with slides of all the different breasts he can make you. I find this part highly suspicious as the slides are of completely naked women in sexual poses. (Dr Jutman at that point told me to remove my pants: I refused, and I know that's why he made my right boob a quarter inch higher than my left . . . also they both look vaguely Japanese.) It has been reported that Dr Jutman keeps women's nipples after the operation . . . I personally think he sells them on the side as cuff links . . . that is why I give him absolutely no stars.

DR ALAN M^CMILLAN – *Stomachs.* (no stars) I would classify Dr McMillan as the Mengele of the cosmetic surgery world. Your stomach does disappear, but so does your naval, and you're left with a slot across your middle which is fine if you're a mail box.

DR MAX KOLHLER – *Face lifts.* ★ His only claim to fame is that he was at Lillian Gish's 88th birthday party and happened to be around when her face started to slide off. He quickly pronged it back on her head with a fork to keep it in place, and has had a following ever since. To me his lifts are too extreme, his patients' faces are so tight you can play bongos on their temples and they look as if they're permanently saying 'Cheese'. A surgeon to be missed.

Dr MARTIN REEVES – *Nose jobs.* ★★★★ Dr Reeves is the Yves St Laurent of the nose world. From the moment he breaks your nose with a hammer you know you're in the hands of an artist. You can actually feel him creating something truly Aryan out of something embarrassingly ethnic. The result

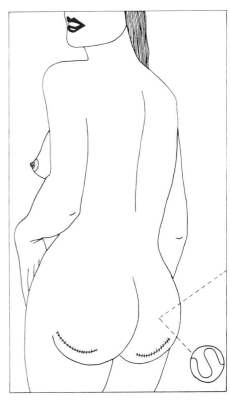

KOLHLER FACE LIFT

REEVES NOSE JOB

BEFORE   AFTER

just screams, 'Hitler youth'. He also believes in the 'natural nose-job' method. No more hospital and nurses: he comes straight to your home and you can have it done while watching TV. When he's finished, he delicately explains that you'll probably look like a runny pizza for the next three months and not to be too alarmed, it's normal.

Dr DONALD BOMASH – *Bottoms.* ★★★ This man gives the highest bottoms known to women. My aunt had hers done and says it's so high up on her whenever she turns around she feels like she's climbing the Himalayas. Also a Bomash bottom is so hard you can rebound tennis balls on it and there was a case where a man pinched a Bomash bottom and broke his fingers. Dr Bomash models his behinds on the Ghauna tribeswomen who can hold up to seven children on their behinds while cooking or picking fruit. Since I've had a Bomash bottom my arms have never gotten tired from carrying my shopping. Also I like his stitchwork . . . both my scars seem to be smiling.

BOMASH BOTTOM

DR JENNIFER ANSWERS YOUR QUESTIONS

Does everybody have them?   *What do they do?*

Where do I put them?   *How big should they be?*

Bosoms are nothing to worry about really, everybody has them, even men have bosoms but theirs don't grow, they just have the teats. Bosoms are the lumps on your front that grow to a variety of sizes on girls, so don't worry if you have noticed them and not known what they were. Most people have just the two on the front, this is what we call 'normal' and they are positioned in the space between your chin and your tummy. If you have more than two this is not normal and you may have to see a doctor and get a special bra made.

If your bosoms grow you can be sure you are a girl and it is perfectly normal. Have a good look at your mother, ask her to stand still for a second so you can look at her bosoms – she won't mind and will understand that you are just worried and curious. If your mother won't let you look at her bosoms ask an older friend or sister, it is best to try it with someone you know and not just to stop any old person on the street or on the bus.

Once you are sure you are growing bosoms there is the question of what to do with them. 'Where shall I put them?' you may well ask. The answer is in bras. Bras are made specially for putting bosoms in, and you can buy them in a variety of shops near where you buy pants.

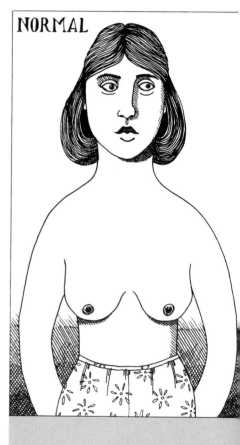

NORMAL

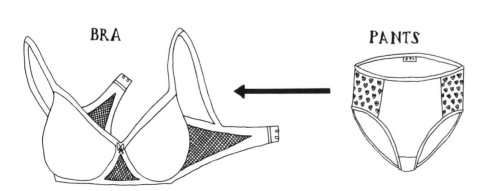

BRA

PANTS

What are they?

Why do I have them?

All these questions and everything you wanted to know answered here.

STRANGE

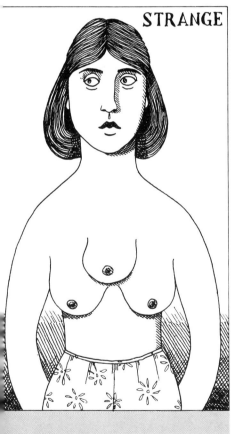

Egg cup

Tea cup

Cereal bowl

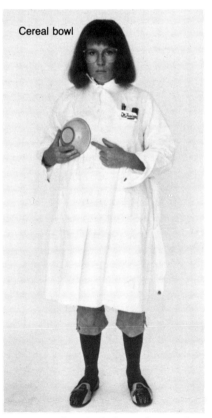

Fruit bowl

You need to find the right size bra for your bosoms so try some on. The size of your bosom is called your 'cup'. So when you go to buy a bra they may say 'what kind of cup have you got?' Some people have small cups like egg-cups or bigger ones like tea cups or coffee mugs. Amanda says I have fruit bowls.

Try a few on – see which fits your bosom best

If you get the wrong cup bra a variety of things can occur.

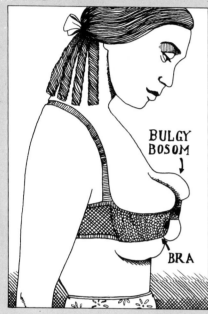

BULGY BOSOM

BRA

Check your bosoms occasionally in case they have grown and you have the bulgy's without knowing. There are no written rules as to how big your bosoms should be: here are some examples of people with different size bosoms.

Dolly Parton – large bosoms
Barbara Woodhouse – large saggy bosoms (could be with a better bra)
Amanda – large bosoms – no bra
Shelley – small bosoms – padded bra
Candice – very high up medium-sized pushed-together bosoms
Princess Anne – Coffee cups – strong bra to stop them wobbling when she's trotting
Marti Caine – tiny egg-cups – bony bosoms
Terry Wogan – just teats

Depending on the size of your bosoms they can be known by a variety of names. They can be Bazookas, big

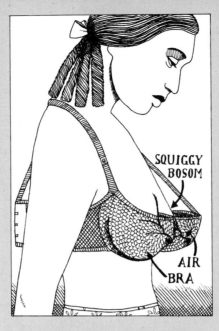

SQUIGGY BOSOM

AIR BRA

ones, Bristol Cities, or Queens Park Rangers, whoppers, and beetroots or tiny ones, fried eggs, poached eggs, scrambled eggs and omelettes, or melons, bananas, hazelnuts, coconuts (must be hairy ones – ugh!) courgettes, cabbages, baked beans and seed potatoes.

So you can see they are very easy things to bring up in everyday conversation. You can have quite a funny time talking about bosoms. When someone says they fancy eating some baked beans I just burst out laughing.

This is all very well I hear you say but 'What are bosoms there for?' Well it's quite simple and nothing to worry about – you FEED BABIES WITH THEM – They are your udders and have milk in them that babies like to drink through the hole in your teats. If you wish to feed a baby it is best to wait until you are asked to do so. Some mothers don't like it if you just walk up to their crying baby and try and put your bosom in its mouth. So best not to try that really, and wait till you get a baby of your own, and they are not easy to come by I know, but more of that another time.

Here is a small poem I made up to end on.

Bosoms are just two lumps
Some have pyramids, some have bumps
But either way do not despair
Cos now you know just why they're there.

People have always had bosoms, so they must always have needed to have bras. But let us ask ourselves how the ancient people made them, if indeed they bothered. Stone Age Ancient people had a troubled time. They began by just propping the bosoms on stone walls when they got tired. But this was simply not practical so they tried making bras to enable more women to move away from the walls. This proved quite

BOSOM

dangerous, the stone bras proved to be too heavy and often the cups would drop on their feet. Some women gave up and let their bosoms sag, until they looked like long deflated sausage

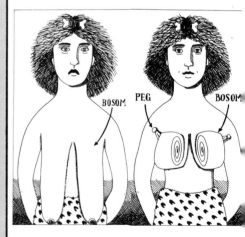

BOSOM   PEG   BOSOM

Saggy bosoms   Bosoms with peg

balloons and they could roll them up and clip them in place with a peg.

But once material had been invented the whole thing became easier, although it took a long time to get to the bra as we know it today.

A SHORT HISTORY OF BRAS THROUGH THE AGES

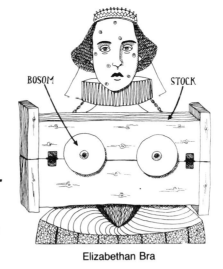

Elizabethan Bra

BOSOM · STOCK

STONE BRA

STONE PANTS

Victorian Bra
(The Crutch Bra)

Ankle-strap

CRUTCH · BOSOM

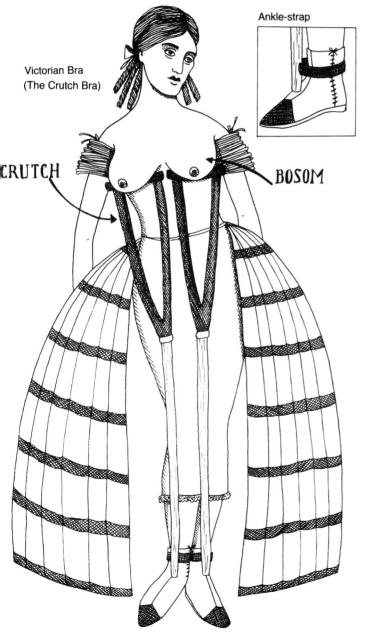

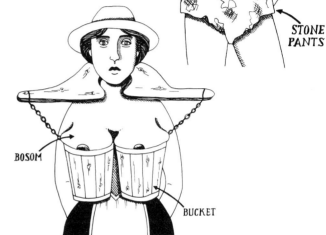

BOSOM · BUCKET

Georgian Bra

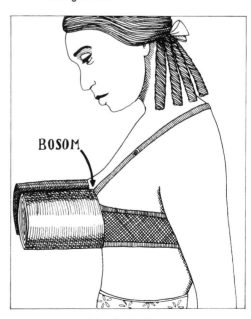

BOSOM

A Bra for the Future

Good for growing bosoms. You need never change your bra size. P.S. I invented this one!

AMANDA'S HOUSEHOLD TIPS

SHOES

Always make sure that someone polishes and cleans your shoes, top and bottom. After all . . .

'A clean bright shoe
Means a whole new you,
Scooby dooby dooby dooby dooby doo . . .'

The endless problem with wearing good, sensible, walking and gripping shoes (which are the most vital part of any serious protesters' uniform) is that of course you do tend to take on board any little gutterside friends. The best way to get rid of dog shit is with a common old kitchen fork. Ensure that someone gouges it all out for you before you go and tread it into the carpets, because that just makes life harder for them again, doesn't it?

They should always either wash away offending matter down kitchen sink with hot water, or scrape onto tissue and flush in usual receptacle – and *please* use rubber gloves, everybody.

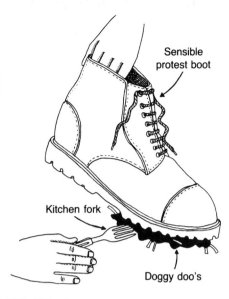

Sensible protest boot

Kitchen fork

Doggy doo's

'I MARRIED MR MUSCLES AND NOW I SPEND MY NIGHTS WITH HIS FATHER AND I'M PREGNANT WITH ANOTHER WOMAN'S CHILD'

BY C. VALENTINE

When I first met Lance, he was the kind of guy every women yearns for, he had a build that just wouldn't quit, it just kept on growing bigger, stronger, longer. He managed a gym in town called 'Hunkers', and I remember how he laughed when I told him that I worked in a wool shop. 'Wool's nice', he told me, 'But I prefer sheep.' And then he picked me up and planted a rough wet kiss on the end of my nose. From that day on he called me wet button nose, and oh, how my heart raced every time I heard that nickname!

It was wonderful for me that summer, spending most afternoons in the gym watching the boys sweat and work up a lather. To watch their big arms flexing and their tight buttocks clenching, I sometimes came over all faint at the thought of their . . .

Continued p27

My night at the Beverly Hills Medical Center

ACTORS' EMERGENCY WARD

OR THE NIGHT I MET ONE HUNDRED STARS

By Shelley Dupont

I had been doing a scene from *Charlie's Angels*, playing Nellie, the waitress. I only had one line, 'More coffee hon?', but Bud was pushing me hard. 'Give me more, Shelley! Show me Nellie's inner core.' It was then I snapped . . . I started to primal scream as Nellie and couldn't stop. The next thing I knew was waking up at the Beverly Hills Medical Centrer – Actors' Emergency Ward under the care of Dr Welby. (They all use TV pseudonyms). He said I had only hyperventilated, but put me on a valium drip and gave me a tummy tuck just to be sure.

Anyway, in recovery I met everyone who's anyone. Shelley Winters was in the bed next to mine. She had overdosed on pastrami sandwiches. They broke six stomach pumps trying to drain her 'cause they kept clogging with cole-slaw. When she finally came to, I tried to engage her in a conversation, but she just belched at me and complained about wind. She did manage to bark that she didn't appreciate people calling her overweight. I said, 'Not overweight, Shel, fat's the word they use. We're talking "Elephant Woman".' She started bubbling so they had to wheel her away.

Then guess what? Red lights flashed, sirens started and all doctors were called to emergency . . . the doors flew open and there she was. Joan Collins was carried in on a stretcher, smoking a cigarette and sucking in her stomach all at the same time. They rushed her into surgery and we all paced for hours waiting to hear the diagnosis. Stephanie (*Hart to Hart*) Powers said she heard rumours that Joan had swallowed a $50,000 diamond merely to prove she's not just physically gorgeous, but has a lot going for her on the inside too. What a bitch! Then four surgeons came out, tearing off their rubber gloves and face masks. They were drenched in sweat.

It was a success. Joan had chipped her fourth right-hand fingernail, but they managed to save it with glue. We all cheered and broke open the champagne. In the middle of the celebrations, Rock Hudson was wheeled in, but the doctors told him to come back later – they were too drunk. Rock was wheeled out and we never saw him again. It couldn't have been important.

What a night! My autograph book was overflowing and it was definitely worth the five figure bill I was slapped with in the morning. As I was leaving, I clipped off my two longest nails and made a speech about starting a Joan Collins fund in case she ever broke one of hers again. I had donated my best and I hoped everyone would follow my example.

As I exited to thunderous applause, I threw Liza Minelli a meaningful sneer, indicating she was on her way down the showbiz toilet bowl and I was perched on the threshold of being 'hot'.

HAVING FUN WITH POTATO

Ilya Kuryakin Potato*

Joan Collins Potato

Little & Large Potato

Now for some alternatives:-

Duncan Goodhew Potato

Princess Anne Potato
(my favourite)

Bonny Langford Radish

MEN

Potatoes and other vegetables can be great fun. Have a look at some of my favourite personalities which I made from potatoes and things:-

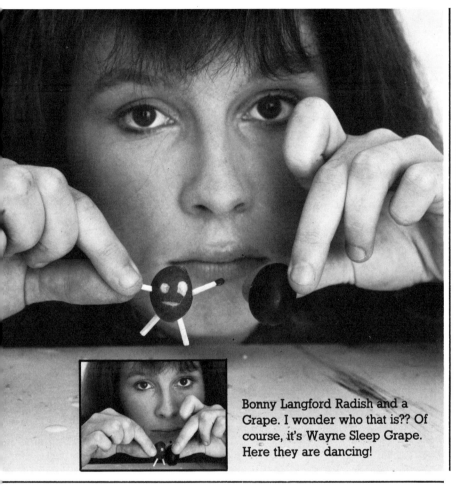

Queen Mother Potato

Cyril Smith Potato

Bonny Langford Radish and a Grape. I wonder who that is?? Of course, it's Wayne Sleep Grape. Here they are dancing!

Jasper Carrot
(sorry, I had a quick nibble)

Queen Mother Olive

So you see there is great fun to be had making them. Then you can have even more fun making up stories for them, and conversations.

e.g. Cyril Smith Potato – 'Hello, Queen Mother, you're very old.'

Queen Mother Potato – 'Yes, Cyril. And you're very fat, aren't you?'

Hilarious!!

GROW YOUR OWN ☆DIAMOND!

In just two weeks with the minimum amount of gardening you can GROW YOUR OWN GENUINE DIAMOND-TYPE STONE.
Yes, this unique product has been scientifically researched in our own secret Swiss laboratories by fully-trained experts.
Since the Pharaohs were buried with their ancient scrolls, no one has been able to fathom one of nature's greatest gifts to mankind.
But with my Egyptian background and endless searching in the tombs of the Nile, I discovered the hieroglyphic parchment that gave the Swiss experts their vital clue. Now you too can share in the ancient mystery.
Give this amazing gift to your friends or to yourself. This priceless gem is within everyone's financial reach. Just plop this 'ordinary looking' seed in any dirt-filled container, sit back and watch your fortune blossom.

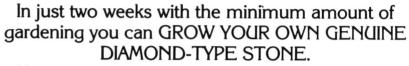

My Bud Years

Bud showing me his well-lenaon "give give give" method.

This is a lock of Bud's hair. He wears a toupee so he didn't feel it when I ripped it out. I stroke it sometimes knowing that it lived close to Bud's brain.

Here I am holding a part of my tooth. I chipped it when Bud was supposed to catch me during our trust exercises. (It didn't matter as it was a cap)

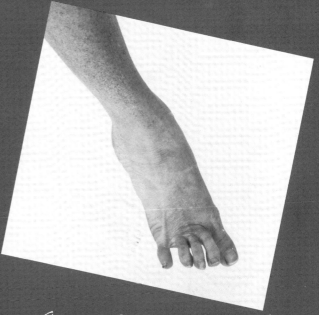

This is the first part of my body that became another character's. Here my foot has become the foot of Mary Tyler Moore.

Stills from my work at Bud's

Me as Shelley Winters in "Poseidon Adventure".
(had to hang for two hours)

Me in Bud's version of "Splash".

Me as "Nonny" the monopede, blind girl
who becomes an international golfer
in "Wheres that ball" (An original by Bud)

Me as 'a dorsal fin' in Bud's version of
"Moby Dick". (My early years, when
I played minor roles)

The Method of Methods!!

NEW ACTING TECHNIQUE SWEEPING THE WESTERN WORLD AND BEYOND!!!

Bud Stanislovsky (Fully Qualified Florist and Actor) has come up with a revolutionary new acting technique that's just buzzing around Beverly Hills. Bud says, 'Learn to act in just eight, yes, eight years. Start tomorrow: eight years later, presto, you're acting.

Author of 'Sir Larry 'n' Me', 'Techniques of Public Masturbation' and 'Flower Arrangements For The Home and Office'.

With the Bud Stanislovsky method your wildest fantasies come true . . .

All you've ever dreamt about show business can now happen . . . the dinner parties, the 'everyone in the Jacuzzi' nights, the affairs with your leading man/woman/both, the expensive drugs and most of all the ability to get a good table at prestigious restaurants . . . all of it with just eight, yes, eight years worth of simple E-Z-to-follow acting training.

Learn the secrets behind the stars: how to fire your agent, how to get the best dressing room, how to walk off set effectively and get results, etc.

Within a few short weeks you'll be able to emote anywhere, anytime without embarrassment . . . within five years you'll represent truth and beauty . . . and by year eight you'll be awarded an official 'I'm a B.S. thespian' degree and several telephone numbers of important show business contacts and close friends of agents.

This dynamic and perfectly legal technique can be at your fingertips for only $25,000.00 including snacks, free parking, and Bud's personal emotional support. The academy is located just off the San Jose highway exit ramp so it's easy so get to. A sidewalk leads you straight to the building which has been freshly painted – with toilet facilities for both men and women.

The snack area has authentic formica table tops and Bud's beautiful, recently constructed (but based on 'The Globe') theatre has a stage and chairs (all facing the same way) and a very clean dressing room.

Bud's classes include:

Insights into the 'Give, give, give method'
'Public humiliation'

Bud's other faculty members include:

Al Stanislovsky B.S.B.S. dancersize master and tarot reader (your future in show biz revealed)

Margo Stanislovsky M.U.R.D. classes: 'Radiating from your innards', 'Magic of the wondrous orifice' and 'Ecstasy of Beingness'

Bucky Stanislovsky L.S.P.D. what-to-do-with-your-hands coach, wigs, and crisis controller.

Chuck Stanislovsky H_2O. Tongue and trauma trainer, 'Acting on turf' seminar.

Tear off here, fill out and send in a self-addressed envelope (Don't forget to put on the stamp) to:

THE BUD (be a star in eight years) STANISLOVSKY ACADEMY c/o STAN STANISLOVSKY STAN'S CAR AND BODY REPAIR SHOP 188 EL DORO ROAD ENCINO CALIFORNIA 90078

I enclose $25,000.00 (Check or money order only)

I wish to go on the Pay-as-you-perform scheme, plus interest

Requirements for entry . . .
Please fill in father's income or personal assets $_____

CHECK ONE
☐
☐

'You won't regret it, I didn't and I'm Meryl Streep'

Notes from the Genius

"NOTES FROM THE GENIUS" - from the diaries of Shelley Dupont
                                    B. S. thespian.

September 14, 1976 Only been on the course one week and had my first nervous breakdown. Bud said this was a good sign.

December 15, 1976 Bud has taken a simple heiress and stripped her bare. Today Bud removed my bronzed-tan base, my mascara and my lip gloss ... had my second nervous breakdown. I was naked in the world and couldn't cope ... all my facial flaws exposed!!! I screamed and screamed and screamed until Bud said my vehicle was empty. He then smiled and said he could now begin to blow art into me. The man is inspired.

April 24, 1977 Bud took us all to an open field today for trauma class. First he blew a whistle and we had to scamper around like nymphs and fairies. "Come on dazzle me, you bitches" he shouted. Then he pulled a gun on us and held us up. Bud got my gold "I love shopping" necklace, my Cartier watch, the keys to my BMW, my cash and the credit cards. I didn't even have money left for a taxi. Had to take public transportation home ... I barfed twice on the bus ... I had heard of them, but never actually had to get on one with all the poor people.

May 14, 1977 Six weeks have gone by and still no sign of Bud.

May 20, 1977 Got a postcard from Bud today from the Bahamas. He says he's fine and that the reason behind the hold-up was to teach us we should never trust anyone in show business ... everyone tries to rob you blind and we might as well learn it the hard way. Bud works in mysterious ways sometimes.

September 28, 1978 Bud did it again. We haven't been getting any snacks lately. We asked Bud where's the cookies and coke, and he showed us the prospectus for the school. Next to "Free snacks", it says in tiny print, "Only on Buddhist holidays". Bud says this is a lesson for us to always read the small print. "If I don't screw you in here, they'll screw you out there."

February 17, 1979 Bud talked today about the importance of being the center of attention. Even with no lines you should be able to take the focus (e.g. the guy who fell under his chariot in "Ben Hur": "We remember him and not the arena sweeper"). The Bud method for getting the focus is standing in front of everyone else and talking the loudest. It's simple, but it works. Bud made us all go on stage and blew his whistle to see which of us could get to the front center the fastest. Luckily I had my nail file with me so I did really well.

October 23, 1979 Bud said we could begin to start character work. He instructed us
to get into one another's skin and turned out the lights. When he turned back on the
lights we were all wearing one another's fur coats. Bud left the room saying that was
not what he meant - tomorrow he'd try again.

December 12, 1980 Bud jogs into class and blows out his everyday personality with a
scream. With a sharp intake of breath he becomes art itself. "theater-in-a-body" he
says to describe himself. He raises a bullhorn to his lips and shouts out names of
emotions at us. Here's some of my best work ... I can change emotions at the rate of
1.7 seconds.

I usually have to put my face in an ice bucket after ten or more of these.

January 25, 1981   Learned to stretch our orifices today ... starting with the main
hole ... the mouth. Bud filled my mouth with as many ping pong balls as possible and
then measured the radius with his bud-ometer. I had the biggest span, 4 2/3 inches
from side-to-side. I told him I was worried about over-stretching 'cause when I close
my mouth, my lips sag below my chin and I've got stretch marks on my cheeks. Tomorrow
Bud says we'll be learning to create an echo with our anal passages.

April 3, 1982 Did actual scene work today for first time. I did a scene from "Charlie's
Angels" playing "Nelly" the waitress and Bud himself played Farrah. He was totally
convincing with just a plain old broom on his head. He enters the coffee shop where I
work and says, "what d' ya' got, Nelly?" I say, "Eggs". Bud neutralizes, so he's Bud
again and screams, "NO, no, no, your 'eggs' tells me nothing about you. What do you
think of eggs? Who are you? Do you have any PETS? Are they house-trained or do they
just pee anywhere?" So many questions I never asked myself. Bud says I was just any
waitress, not "Nelly, the waitress". So Bud starts what he calls 'breaking someone
down' by screaming at me, "Your mother's a whore and your father's a crook". He then
makes me say "Eggs" again and it sounds roughly the same. Bud then whispers, "You
have a pimple on your nose," and that's it: I crack. I break down in floods of tears
and almost choke to death as I say, "Eggs". Everyone in the class applauds wildly
and Bud whispers to me, "You don't really have a pimple," but it's too late, I've
gone into shock. Bud has to phone an ambulance and I'm rushed to the Beverly Hills
Medical Center, Actors' Emergency Ward. Bud sends me a telegram reading, "You now
truly understand Nelly, bravo, bravo, kiss, kiss, Bud" I am becoming a thespian - I
can feel it.

May 4, 1984 Bud came into class today dressed as the 'the Bard' with a full ruffled
collar and a goatee beard. (He just used his toupee on his chin I think, 'cause he
was bald for the first time). He said we would attempt the classics but first we had
to get over our middleclass hang-ups. (Or in my case, way above middleclass) He said
you couldn't do Lady Macbeth and worry about under-arm stains or spit coming out of
your mouth, so today we would concentrate on losing our inhibitions and then he belched
at us without blusing ... Bud is such proof of the pudding. So we all went to a
restaurant and had to do what Bud calls his 'public humiliation exercises'. Didi stood
on the table and covered herself with pizza sauce while singing "Buffalo Gal". Sandy
showed us all her cellulite deposits. It was gross. Then I got up and peed on the menu.
Bud gave me full marks and said I was ready to do Shakespeare.

June 30, 1984 Graduation day today. I can't believe it, eight years have just zoomed
by. We all had to do a final performance for Bud and the staff. I did "Sal", Rhoda's
neighbor from "Rhoda" - the scene where she borrows the Ketchup, but I jabbed my
finger in my eye during a dramatic gesture, so had to stop. Then everyone in the class
sang "Jesus Christ Superstar" but substituted Jesus with Bud's name. There was a special
award-giving ceremony: Bud gave me the "Biggest car in the parking lot" award. He then
handed out our B. S. thespian degrees, a cardboard gold star for our first dressing room
and the telephone number of a show business contact, but said the number might have
changed, he got it a while ago. I started screaming I wasn't ready to work without
Bud ... I still needed his guidance. Bud slapped me across the face - told me I was
obviously meant to be a classical actress and I should go to London, quickly. He would
chip in for the fare. With my emotional state, he said, I should be playing the big
neurotics. Then he left as fast as he entered that theatrical but plain, yellowish
building. I said my final farewell to the snack bar ... so many memories ... the bitching,
the nerves, the egg salad sandwiches. It was then I had MY LAST NERVOUS BREAKDOWN at
the Bud Stanislovsky Academy and my mother had to carry me home in a bag.

PRESS RELEASE . . . PRESS RELEASE . . . PRESS RELEASE . . . PRESS RELEASE . . . PRESS RELEASE . . .

THE BEVERLEY HILLS BROWSER

LAST NIGHT Shelley Dupont gave us her one-woman show, 'Babs – An Evening With. A close scrutiny of the esteemed career of Barbra Streisand.' Shelley took us from Barbra's beginnings, humming to herself behind a deli counter in Brooklyn through the day she decided she had an interesting nose instead of a big honker, right up to her magnificent performance as that Yiddish drag artist, Yentl. We wept with Babs . . . like the time her home in Malibu flooded. We laughed with her like when she decided to have sex with her hairdresser. We ate with her . . . Shelley served some of Barbra's favorite foods during the show; egg rolls and tuna melts. But her finest moment was when she lip sang 'The Way We Were' to a cardboard cutout of Robert Redford. At the end of the three and a half hours Shelley made everyone stand on stage arm-in-arm as she did the classics 'People' and 'Don't Rain on My Parade' in hand signals for the deaf. Only Shelley Dupont has the width of character to fully encompass Miss Streisand's enormous persona and we thank her for the homage paid. Two big, big legends coming out of one mouth.

SHELLEY DUPONT

Acting Experience Since Graduating

August 4, 1979 — *Role* – 'Screaming woman, wearing dacron' in an industrial film about allergies caused by synthetic fibers.

November 14, 1982 — *Role* – 'Screaming camper' in an industrial film about blowing out matches when in a tent.

February 21, 1984 — *Role* – 'Screaming unseatbelted driver' in an industrial film about driving without a seatbelt while eating a hamburger.

I also auditioned for 'Annie' seven times, but they said I was too tall.

THE BEVERLY HILLS SHOPPER

REVIEWS

Sheer audacity and utter ▓▓▓▓▓ Shelley Dupont's performance last night at the 'Bud Stanislovsky Rib 'n' Chicken Dinner Playhouse of Performing Thespians'. Ms Dupont played 'Buffy', the Ali McGraw role in 'Love Story' and was ▓▓▓▓▓ relentless vivaciousness knew no bounds ▓▓▓▓▓ insisted on skipping throughout the play ▓▓▓▓▓ unbelievable. ▓▓▓▓▓ sickmaking. Ms Dupont felt she didn't need the script and improvised her role to the horror of her fellow actors ▓▓▓▓▓ The audience were struck dumb when she said, 'The good news is I'm a pregnant preppie, the bad is I've got leukemia, sorry.' And at that point, for some unknown reason, she threw her head back and let out a blood-curdling wail of such abnormal velocity that her startled co-star's last line, 'Love is never having to say you're sorry', was rendered unheard. In my mind that's when the show really ▓▓▓▓▓ because Ms Dupont spent the rest of the evening refusing to die. She sobbed around the stage bidding a hysterical farewell to every prop on the set, clutching a coffee table, weeping uncontrollably, gagging and spluttering 'I'll never use you again, good-bye' ▓▓▓▓▓ stage manager finally had to hit her over the head to stop the show. ▓▓▓▓▓ pathetic ▓▓▓▓▓ raving tragic performance ▓▓▓▓▓ never again.

Al Burnbomb

The Kandy Kross

Candice Valentine brings you God's lovely prezzie to Mankind, created by 'HIM' for the world. Product sent from heaven, absolutely *not* made by human hands.

TOTALLY UNBELIEVABLE . . . STRANGER THAN FICTION

Today is the first day of the rest of your life, and everything you ever yearned for, all your hopes and desires *can come true*. All the wealth, happiness and prosperity of your wildest dreams. So many miracles are so easily attainable. All that success you never had, the love that never came your way are now eminently possible. You have always wanted charisma, charm, luck, and money and it is my heartfelt belief that you can have all of this like never before. So much joy.

ARE YOU OLD, UGLY, SPOTTY, FAT AND ALCHOLIC?

The KANDY KROSS is a divine gift made famous by Jesus and brought to you via me. It is NOT a gimmick. It can make you win at the races, slot machines, mirror bingo, sweepstakes, trivial pursuits or other chance games.

I WANT YOU TO HAVE THIS

It has been worn by people who have definitely died and come back to life again, like soldiers for instance.

Incurable cripples have become professional athletes.

SEBASTIAN COE
DALEY THOMPSON

The instant you touch the KANDY KROSS, you'll feel the heat of good luck, health, wealth, good looks and weight loss surging through your entire body.

I can honestly say that if you read this article and do *not* purchase the KANDY KROSS, I cannot be held responsible for any mishaps, bad luck and tragic personal misery.

The Bible so obviously infers . . . 'thou shalt not enter the kingdom of the successful and rich lest thou wearest thine KANDY KROSS'.

DO YOU WANT YOUR FAMILY TO LIVE???!!!

'Since wearing the KANDY KROSS, I have become a millionaire and lost 5 stone in excess weight.' . . . Mr T. Smith, a miner from Harrogate.

■■■■■■■■■■■■■■ no-risk, genuine guaranteed coupon ■■■■■■■■■■■■■■

YES, I WANT EVERYTHING IN LIFE, SO PLEASE SEND ME

▢ KANDY KROSSES

BY RETURN OF POST

BOX NO 599, LONDON S.W. 10

CHOICE OF COLOURS: PINK, MAUVE, SEE-THROUGH

BOOKS I HAVE READ AND RECOMMEND HIGHLY

(quite a lot of them are only available in that small shop 'Lesbos' in Camden)

Lisa Alterego – OTHER WOMEN MIGHT DO IT TOO
About the female predicament, and who to blame, mainly Dr Whites.

Sausage Writerberg – A GIRLS' ADVENTURE STORY
When Beccy and Maureen fall into a volcano by accident, their families give them up for dead. This is the story of their long, hard, uphill struggle . . . for plastic surgery.

Mz C. Jealous – WHY JOAN COLLINS IS A PERFECT BITCH
An in-depth look at Mz C's feelings.

Gertie Fairbottom – THE SISTERS OF BROTHERS
'Brothers' is a fictional planet where the men have babies and the women don't. An hilarious and biting satire.

Eve Ho – THE BOBBIN' WOMEN
Not, as you might imagine (well, I did) a story about cross-channel swimmers. No, it's something to do with lace. I didn't quite finish it, but some needle-women might find it compelling, I suppose.

Vagina Spittle – WOMEN'S PARTS
A fascinating book about the part women played in the archeological dig for Mrs Tutankhamun's mummified breasts, buried separately from the rest of her body.

Ma Earthy – RUSSIAN WOMEN
A bitter-sweet novel about how fast women have to move around.

A QUICKIE

SPOT THE DIFFERENCE

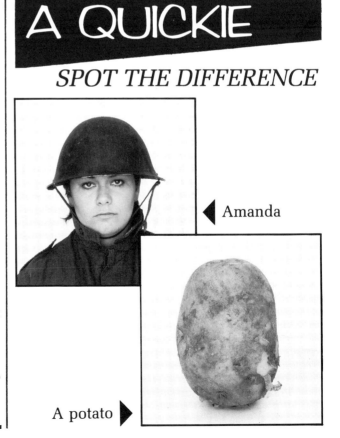

◀ Amanda

A potato ▶

Candice's Map of the World

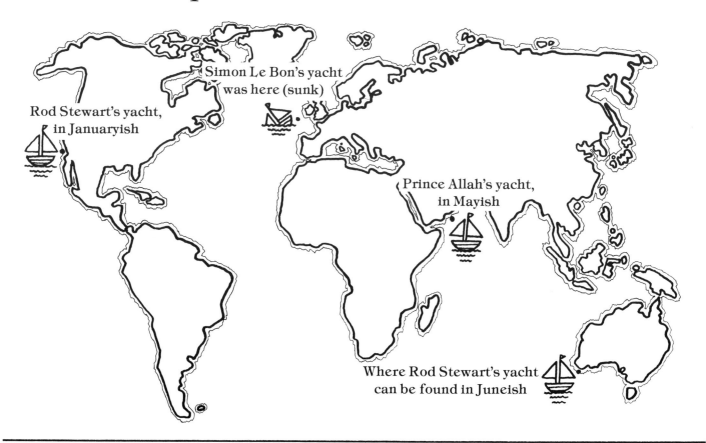

MAP OF THE WORLD (By Jennifer)

LADY CARLTON'S NOCTURNAL ACCESSORIES

The Filter - a protection against nocturnal germs

The AC/DC - an artificial means for divine inspiration

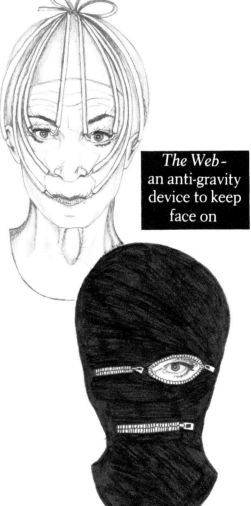

The Web - an anti-gravity device to keep face on

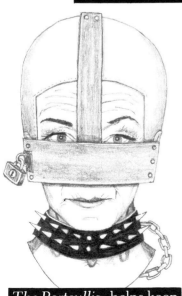

The Portcullis - helps keep useful juices escaping

The Shergar - keeps the world steadied and focused during hangover period

The Peek-a-boo Hood - good for full facial skin tightening

Gypsy Valentine's ASTROLOGICAL ASSESSMENT

NAME: AMANDA RIPLEY

AGE: 25 Yrs

EXACT DATE OF BIRTH: 2nd OCT 1960

TIME OF DAY: 2.15ish

BREAST FED?: YES/NO

WEIGHT AT BIRTH: no comment, but definitely healthy, lots of hair.

FINGERPRINT:

PERSONALIZED ASTROLOGICAL CHART:

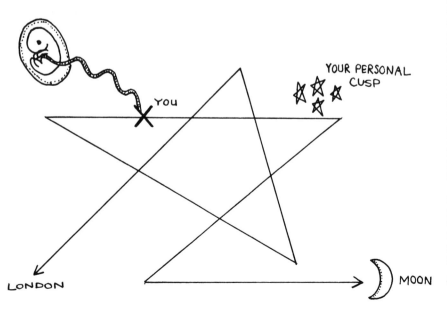

YOU ARE A LIBRAN

YOUR LUCKY NUMBER: 4

YOUR LUCKY STONE: CRYSTAL

TODAY'S PREDICTION: Possibility of abnormal weather: beware of hazardous gadgets.

YEAR'S PREDICTION: This year, mercury will be travelling through Uranus, so avoid cheesy substances.

CHART ANALYSIS:
When the moon is in the seventh house,
And Jupiter aligns with Mars,
Then peace will guide our planet,
And love,
Love will steer the stars.
This is the dawning of the age of
Aquarius, Mand..
The age of Aquarius, aaaahhhhh.

As you can see, Mand., I have no control over your stars, I'm just the voicepiece here on earth interpreting their twinkling message. This is what they tell me, Mand. (remember, I'm not saying this, they are): . . . you are an overly dominant person who bosses around those near to you . . . flatmates maybe? Being a Libran with a very large cusp indicates to me that your aggressive behaviour is due to sexual frustration, which might be linked to the fact that you haven't had many boyfriends in your life. Since there is a definite eclipse in your Venus, you may discover that you're a teeny bit bisexual. Well, better than nothing, right, Amanda?

My advice is to experiment with your sexuality, Mand., not at home because there people don't really want to be involved or witness it. Go out a lot. Wash that hair for a change, and try to get laid, eh? Then you might wake up to find yourself a nicer person to live with – who knows?

OTHER LIBRANS: Mussolini, Eva Braun, Billy Jean King, Hattie Jacques.

Price for full beauty assessment
£102 + VAT + expenses
£178.28
PAID IN FULL

Madame Candice's Personal Beauty Assessment

NAME: SHELLEY DUPONT

AGE: IRRELEVANT (but flawless, apparently)

COMMENTS:

1. Oh dear, I wouldn't want to be your comb, Shelley, no chance of getting out alive!! Far too much henna, Shel., we can all tell – the bathroom towels match your hair, whoops!

2.

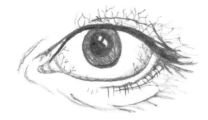

Don't give us that old 'they add to my character' nonsense Shel. – any more crows' feet and people will mistake your face for a map of the underground.

3. Oh, so that's where I parked my articulated lorry!

4. They don't call you 'old accordian neck' for nothing, Shel. You know what they say about trees – every ring represents ten years – well, by my calculations next year is your bicentennial. As for the chins . . . gobble, gobble . . .

5. Boobies – missing.

6. Tummy. Well done, Shelley, for not caring what people think. Perhaps those boobies are hidden in here somewhere.

7. Bottom. Shelley, you could stretch out those cheeks and go hang-gliding!

8. Bikini Line. Let's weed that jungle foliage . . . oh, oh, found a nest of cuckoos! (Interesting that this growth is a different colour to head area, see over-dyed hair 1.)

9. Legs. A super, funny impression of a Jew's harp.

OVERALL IMPRESSION:

Plenty of work to be done here, but don't give up hope. Did you know that every seven years we shed our skins and get a whole new set of cells? Hopefully, you'll be luckier next time around.

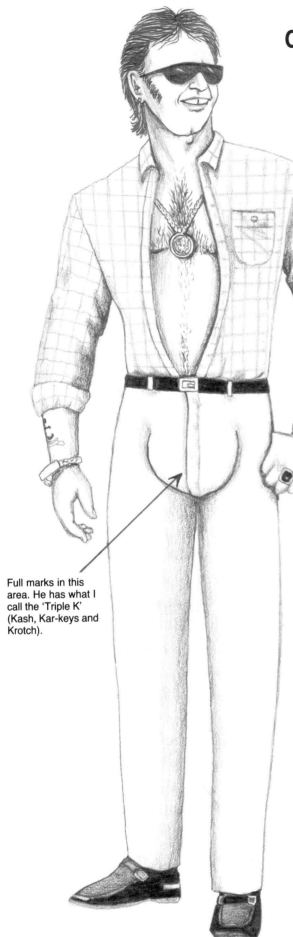

Full marks in this area. He has what I call the 'Triple K' (Kash, Kar-keys and Krotch).

CANDICE VALENTINE – SEXOLOGIST
FRONT AND REAR ADVICE AND INSTRUCTION

HOOKING MR RIGHT

Girls, what are we all after? We're all after the real thing. And the real thing in my book has the gold American Express card (not Access), the Porsche (not the Capri), and bikini Y-fronts (not jockey shorts).

A bar or disco is usually where you'll find him. Once you've got him in range take aim and fire.

CANDICE VALENTINE'S HANDY TIPS FOR SNATCHING YOUR MAN

1. Mounting the bar stool. *THE APPROACH* Whilst carefully lifting one cheek onto the stool with your left hand, brush gently against his arm with your boobs. Continue moving the boobs around in a graceful arc until they eventually land on the cocktail counter. (Also put right cheek on stool.) Important: Moisten and pout lips as if blowing a tuba, and say in a husky, breathy, voice, 'Excuse me, kind sir, is there any chance of a meaningful relationship?'

2. If he turns his back, don't be discouraged. Dismount from your stool and approach him from the front.

3. Now's your chance to be playful. Take the straw/cocktail swirler out of his drink and flirtily blow the contents of the straw into his surprised face. Men love a girl with a good sense of humour. While he's still wiping himself down, take the chance to show him that you're not just fun but sexy too. See diagram.

INSTRUCTIONS FOR SEDUCTION WITH A STRAW

Open mouth, swirl the straw around inner lip in clockwise movement, moistening constantly as you go. Fondle and flick straw with tip of protruding tongue. Now he's looking at you! Close mouth on end of straw and begin in and out motion, gradually building up speed.

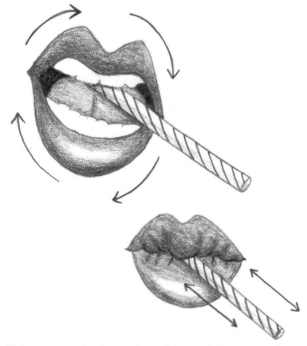

When you feel you've driven him to a frenzy, pull straw out immediately and wait for him to invite you home for 'that cup of coffee'.

THE PENTHOUSE PLAN

RULE ONE: Regress to childhood behaviour and adopt a baby voice. Pretend to be helpless and not understand anything, e.g. the mysteries of hi-fi equipment, dimmer switches, electric curtains and revolving bed. (Phrases I have used successfully in baby talk: 'Vat's vewy clever. Candy likee funny lights. Candy likee touchee ooooooh.')

RULE TWO: Immediately roll on carpet, licking yourself, purring, arching your back and stretching. Wet lips, lower lids and say, 'Grrrrrrr'. As he pounces on you, jump up and exit to bathroom.

RULE THREE: Check medicine cabinet and bathroom thoroughly to see if you're really with Mr Right.

Mr Right's medicine cabinet and bathroom contain	Mr Wrong's medicine cabinet and bathroom contain
Phallic-shaped deodorant	Moisturizer
Aftershaves called anything like 'Beast', 'Turbo' or 'Slash'.	Essence of lime aftershave
Vaseline	Tweezers
Soap on a rope	Baby Powder
Athlete's foot powder	Grecian 2,000
Stack of Playboys	Shower cap
Short black kimono	Non-slip bathmat
Drips on toilet seat	Cotton buds
Champagne toothpaste	Kaftan

Warning! If there is any evidence of other women, flush it immediately down toilet pan and replace with your own accessories.

If you're really sure he's Mr Right, go all the way.

During the night, get answers to the following questions:

1. Is he insured for other people to drive his car?
2. Annual income (gross)
3. Does he enjoy company on business trips?

Before you leave flat, hide one earring under sofa to ensure a return visit.

_____

Other pamphlets available in the Candice Valentine series include:
'Foreplay – the ultimate bargaining tool'
'Using false pregnancy for profit'
'Foot-play for when your hand gets tired'
'Vaseline – a girl's best friend'
'Sound effects for multiple orgasm'

See overleaf for one of my less successful clients –

JENNIFER'S DATE

1. Intense eye contact.

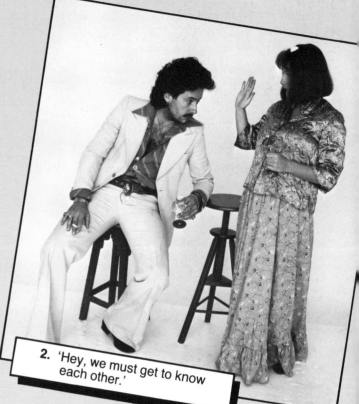

2. 'Hey, we must get to know each other.'

3. Gliding in discreetly.

4. She's so forward!!

5. 'Need a light?'

6. She doesn't smoke.

7. She's so sexy!

8. The look that says it all.

9. That provocatively darting tongue has him well and truly hooked.

10. The preliminaries over.

12. Sure of her man.

11. Going in for the kill.

My Dear Germaine, or shall I call you 'Germ',

(Since I feel we know each other quite well now, after all I have been writing to you for three years now, haven't I?) (Oh, and by the way, I don't mind that you haven't had time to reply, I know that you're extremely busy getting out there and fighting for the right of women to have sex)

I feel compelled to write to you this week concerning a very sensitive issue. I know that you of all people will understand this, Germy, because God knows I'm surrounded by a group of hideously politically retarded women in this flat.

All I'm going to say is: imagine if you knew someone who knew someone who insisted on applying make-up in front of you in the sanctity of your own living room, even after you'd explained about the plight of the she-whale in the North Atlantic, and how thoughtless it is to use their afterbirth to decorate your eyelids ... I mean, what would you do???!!! See what I mean??!!

Despite all this oppression, you'll be glad to hear that I'm staying strong ... Quote "I am Woman, hear me tick..." unquote. ....Actually, talking about quotes, can I just say that I loved that part in your book 'Sex and Destiny' where you said, Quote "This book is dedicated to my cat, Bubbles" unquote. ....That is so true, isn't it? Thank God you're out there, expressing it for all of us. Unfortunately, I haven't been able to read very much of your book as yet due to my heavy (to say the least!!) commitments on 'Spare Cheeks'. Heard of it? - it's a magazine for women, by women, to women, of women, under women, about women, and basically alot of other things to do with women-type things. (See magazine). I wouldn't be at all surprised if you subscribed to it already but just in case you don't, please find latest copy enclosed. Oh, and there's a surprise, I seem to be the major focus on the front cover, don't I?.

Anyway, I do think that 'Sex and Destiny' is a great title for a book which is obviously about feminist astrology .... um .... since I haven't read it yet, I was wondering, could you tell me in advance, am I destined to have any sex soon?... (I was born on 1st April 1957, if it helps).

Yours, in sisterly bondage, *Amanda Ripley* ♀
(Head of Chelsea Sisters in Trouble Support Group)

P.S. At the moment, I'm compiling an article called 'Healthy Vaginas' - Any hints or pictures you could spare?

P.P.S. I've got an uncanny feeling that you and I may be menstruating at the same time. My dates last month were 14-18th - what about you?

P.P.P.S. Isn't it a crime that tampons are subject to 'luxury tax'. I personally don't think that bleeding to death every month for men is a luxury, do you?

Quote "Only Women Bleed" unquote.

SPARE

Cheeks

amanda ripley saves young woman from whale blubber

JENNIFER'S

1. JOIN THE DOTS.

What happens is you must start off with a pen, pencil or biro or anything else that might write and take it in your hand (*or* sometimes you can sharpen up a lipstick). Then with a line join up the dots. I already know what the picture is of as I made it up, but you won't until you've joined them up or read the answer which is at the bottom of the page, upside down as a sort of disguise. Sometimes when you're joining the dots up you might like to guess what it is – this one might be an elephant or a helicopter, I didn't even really know while I was drawing it. I thought 'Oh, Oh! I hope nobody thinks this is an elephant or a helicopter.'

ANSWER SHELLEY

2. SPOT THE DIFFERENCE (15 Differences)

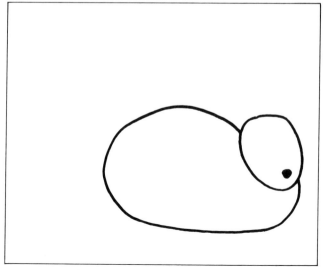

PUZZLER

CROSSWORD

ACROSS

1. A good bready sort of name for Amanda that is on the front of her head (3–4)
5. Not very nice to clean, can be white, blue, or green. (3)
6. It comes from 5 across then goes under the roads where it gives diseases. Then floats into the sea. (8)
7. You get into things and then try to run as fast as you can. A very tricky thing, I normally fall over. (4–4)
9. Take Amanda's name and take out the 'n' then squash the others up and take out the 'A' and then take off the other 'A' and then you've got it. (3)
10. Fill in the missing word. Well known from 'The Sound Of Music',

Doe a dear, a female dear
Me a bit of golden sun
Ray a name I call myself
 ? I've got a long long way to Rome
Far a needle pulling thread
Tea a note follow . . ?
Lard a drink of jam and bread
That will bring us back to do

12. You can kill somebody in it if you don't like them and with very little thought and without even letting them know about it first. You would also have it in your veins and heart if you had been dead a while or were sitting in a fridge. Now take off the first and last letters and put 'p's in their place or else the other clues won't fit. (9)
15. An old friend from home. Our mothers know each other. (6)
16. If someone says a thing to you that you agree with you say it or

if they say 'do you want something' and you say 'the word' you will get it – if they really meant they would give it to you in the first and weren't playing a trick on you, like: 'Jennifer would you like a cup of coffee?'
  'the word'
  'then go and make it yourself then, and make me 2 cups while you're at it.' (3)

DOWN

1. You put them in bras. (6)
2. They are wet but very friendly and have quite a good life really just in ponds or aquariums or sitting on pebbles looking. Remember if you have them as pets to keep them well watered. I had some once and they just went crisp. (5)
3. A word said by magic men or geniuses like Aladin when they want to open something or make something appear without touching it. (11)
4. A pudding made from animals that live in the Arctic and pull sleighs. (5)
5. Sounds a bit like *LENA* (SKINNER) but begins with a different letter. (4)
8. My nickname at school. I don't know where they got it from because it doesn't sound a bit like Jennifer. (5)
11. A very funny man who makes me laugh when he looks at the camera when other people are trying to talk. Quite good looking actually. (5)
12. They are orange, blue, yellow, green and pink. They are not like real ones but you can groom them.
'My . . ?' (4)
(you must be stupid if you don't know this).
13. When you have a thing with a top that is not covered you get them and stick them on. (4)
14. When your mouth isn't sticking up anymore you are this. (3)

JENNIFER'S JOKES

1. Why did the chicken cross the road?
   To avoid bumping into Amanda who was walking down the other side.

2. Knock Knock!
   Who's there?
   Amanda
   Amanda who?
   Amanda Ripley
   Oh no.

3. What's the similarity between a small loaf of bread and Amanda?
   Answer – They both look like buns to me.

4. What's the difference between a lump of old ham with a face painted on it and legs – and Amanda Ripley?
   Answer – Nothing.

Continued from p4

. . . washing, which must have taken so long to do! I secretly knew that Lance was the best – once, just for a dare, he ate some nautilus equipment!! One day, when he was showing a lady body-builder how to hold in her tummy and push out her boobs, he looked over to me. As his eyes caught mine, I felt the colour rising hotly in my cheeks . . . there was a strange sort of weird telepathy. I just knew then that I'd given my heart away, with the possibility of some serious sex later.

We went back to his dormobile and didn't waste any time. The intensity in Lance's face when he ease himself onto . . .

Continued p33

SPOT THE ODD ONE OUT – My Pony and Me

A QUICKIE

If Jack ate 3 apples and Mary ate 6 apples, if Paul ate a banana and Josephine ate an orange. What did Peter eat?

ANSWER: A GRAPE

Tee Hee!!

Ha Ha Ha!

AMANDA'S POSTERS FOR SENSIBLE LIVING

You can make these very cheaply with only paper and one very *thick* black felt tip.

IS IT FAIR OR IS IT <u>NEAT</u> TO FIND SOMEONE ELSES DROPPINGS ON THIS <u>SEAT</u>?

NO, SO PLEASE CLEAN SEAT EVERY TIME YOU USE IT

REMEMBER!

FLUSH BEFORE YOU LEAVE

THEN NO-ONE HAS TO HEAVE

NONE OF US WANT THE BLACK PLAGUE!

SO PLEASE SWEEP UP YOUR CRUMBS OTHERWISE WE'LL BE OVERRUN WITH DISEASE RIDDEN RODENTS IN NO TIME AT ALL

HAVEN'T ANY OF YOU READ CHAUCER?!

THANK YOU

FOR NOT DROPPING ASH ON THE CARPET AND RISKING THE WHOLE HOUSE GOING UP IN FLAMES, KILLING US ALL IN A BLOODY AND TRAGIC ACCIDENT

HAVE YOU BOTHERED TO CHECK RECENTLY WHETHER ANY OF OUR ELDERLY NEIGHBOURS HAVE DIED?! THINK TWICE ABOUT IT!

NEED A LIGHT? YES! SO DO LOTS OF PEOPLE IN SOUTH AMERICA

SO PLEASE SAVE FUEL AND TURN OFF THAT LIGHT BEFORE YOU LEAVE THE ROOM.

IS IT FAIR TO THE UNEMPLOYED THAT WE SHOULD LEAVE OUR WINDOWS OPEN?! <u>NO!!!</u>

SAVE THE WHALE SAY NO TO MAKEUP!

SKY-LARKING KILLS

LOOK OUT! THERE'S AN AGGRESSIVE-LOOKING SUSPICIOUS CHARACTER WITH AN AXE ABOUT

SO PLEASE CLOSE AND LOCK THIS DOOR WHEN LEAVING!

DID YOU GET A CHANCE TO SAY YOUR PRECIOUS PARTING WORDS?
IS THERE ANY MESSAGE YOU'D LIKE TO HEAR?

The Kandy Kall

Telephone spiritualist

Hear the voices of dead loved ones on your own phone!
Be connected to the next world, further than Telecom has ever reached . . . a Hotline to Heaven!
Write to Kandy, Your divine switchboard operator, and 'that' call could reach you any day direct from beyond.

Just fill in the coupon and send your (crossed) cheque to: Kandy Marketing Inc.
Box 599 London S.W.10

■ ■cut here■ ■

I WISH TO SPEAK TO MY DEAD LOVED ONE.

Dead person's name:

Relationship:

Sex:

Accent:

Age:

How died:

General conversation topics:

Details of any special message I'd like to hear:

I ACCEPT THERE MAY BE SOME DISTORTION ON
THE LINE FROM HEAVEN AND ALSO THAT
DUE TO DEATH, THERE MAY BE UNAVOIDABLE
DIFFERENCES IN LOVED ONE'S HEAVENLY VOICE.
PRICE PER MINUTE: 5.00p

My name:

Telephone no:

(Kandy can always leave a divine message on your
ansaphone if you're out.)

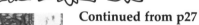

Continued from p27

. . . the sleeping bag beside me, filled me with love and lust. We started slowly, with him gently removing his Y-fronts and pointing to the mattress. But then something primitive happened, and we grew to a crescendo of molten passion, and everything. Me, writhing around with hot lava; and him, an animal-thrashing, lust-driven, maniac. He ejected, lit a cigarette and wiped himself off. It was everything I'd ever dreamed of, and oh, how we laughed.

However, I soon became bored with his constant demand for violent sex in dormobiles parked on double-yellow lines, and the sharp intensity of our first encounter became just a memory. I needed change, I needed variation, I needed something else . . . I needed something different and varied.

That's when I met . . .

Continued p41

USING A TAXI FOR EXERCISE

A lot of people stop me and ask how I have such a fabulous figure: here's my secret.

Hailing the taxi.
(Plenty of arm exercise with this one. Those flabby parts just melt away with constant up and down motion.)

Opening the door.
(Good for a general stretch all over.)

Stepping in.
(Firm thighs and calves as you lift from street level to taxi floor.)

Bending forward to give destination.
(Stomach and waist stay in shape with this movement.)

Watching the meter.
(Calories just evaporate with the anxiety of watching those numbers clock up. Forget about aerobics for building up a sweat and speeding up the heart – this one really gets it pounding.)

Paying the driver.
(Another calorie-dropper as you hand over the green-backs and of course fingers stay supple as you open and close your purse.)

Let Fonda have the heart attack – I get where I'm going and still stay in shape. And as for Racquel Welch, she's got too much surface to clean for my taste.

FROM THE DESK OF
Shelley Dupont

MY NOTES ON HOW TO BREAK INTO SHOW BUSINESS

Approach people who might know famous people or people who might
be connected to 'the biz' anywhere and everywhere.   This is how
a number of stars made it.   Here's me on the streets getting
discovered - I'm giving my medley from "Yentl" to:

Approaching famous person in haste on sidewalk   Famous person in car   (I think)

Ringing famous person's bell   Famous person refused to   Climbing in through window
and singing into ansaphone   answer so went to window   of famous person

FROM THE DESK OF
Shelley Dupont

MY PLAN FOR GETTING INTO NATIONAL THEATER

Went to National and demanded audition, stage-doorman refused
to let me in. (It's always the little people who get in your
way.) Was forced to write a memo announcing my arrival the
following day. (I don't approve of writing, it's so desperate,
but had no choice.) Returned following day and still stopped
by stage-doorman. Waited for Sir McKellen several hours.

Finally jumped him and   Here's me doing my audition.   Went well, I think.
did my "Juliet" piece.

Here's me doing a little self-promotion.

FROM THE DESK OF
Shelley Dupont

MY PLAN FOR BREAKING INTO WEST END SHOW

Picked show I wanted to be in and rented relevant costume.
Bought ticket close to front and during big climax scene leapt
on stage and joined in. Bit stage manager who tried to nab
me, but was pulled off anyway. Had to abort mission.

Me in costume "with cast".   Me buying ticket close to front. A "nobody" escorting me out.

MY PLAN FOR BREAKING INTO FILMS.

Vital to get my face on celluloid. Have been on the look-out
for camera crews. My plan was to listen for ambulances or
fire engines and follow them, then elbow my way to front of
piece.   (I was going to do last scene from "Terms of Endearment"
playing both parts.)

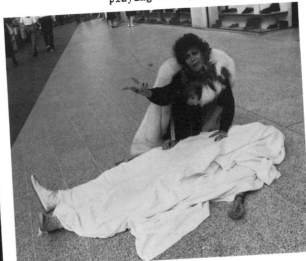 

Have no luck finding a disaster so have
rented a corpse and phoned BBC.

Here's me preparing suitable expression for
when the film crew arrives.

I'M ON!

VAGINA MY OWN

PERIODS (why we suffer, and why we shouldn't feel guilty)

I N THE BEGINNING, when Jesus invented Adam and Eve, a big mistake happened. No one thought to tell Eve not to eat the Golden Delicious, so it was always a trick question. Besides, she knew the old wives' tale that the smell of citrus kept away snakes, so naturally her protective instinct for her man came to the fore, and off she went eating, chomp, chomp, chomp. (Not many people know that she suffered with 'goosegogitis', which is an allergy to green fruit, so she really was being brave.)

Oh yes, it's really easy for God to come down and say, 'Oh dear, you've eaten an apple, therefore you're going to have horrific pains and torrential bleeding from your toilet parts once a month for the rest of your life, as a punishment', isn't it? Thanks, God. Personally, I think Eve had a very sound motive, she should have had a better lawyer.

First of all, I want to say something important about the menstrual cycle . . . yes, it is very important to exercise, and don't let anyone tell you otherwise.

Periods aren't nice, let's face it. However, they are the one thing we all have in common as women: in a way we are a sisterhood united under blood . . . that's the way I like to think of it, anyway. It helps to ease those long lonely hours of writhing agony just before the familiar warm, sticky gush. ('The Curse Of The Red Corpuscle' as I call it.)

Over the years, there have been many nicknames for 'it' most of which have been invented by men who we all know suffer in the main from 'Menstruation Envy'.

Why isn't it called Womenstruation Envy. Eh?!

Here are some of the nicknames . . .

ON BLOB	USING A
ON THE RAG	CYLINDRICAL
SHOWING THE RED	SHAPED COTTON
FLAG	THING TO
HIDING A RED	ABSORB BLOOD
MOUSE	THAT COMES
THE RED NIAGARA	DOWN YOUR
FALLS	VAGINA

Ha, Ha. Very funny, I don't think
Here are some nicknames for boys' Swedish Parts.
You can use any of these as a vicious put-down if any boy gets at you for being 'on'.

ONE-EYED	PENIS
SAUSAGE SNACK	SMELLY WORMY
(or is it snake?)	THING WITH A
THRASHING	HAT ON
DONGER	

BIG MEAT
INJECTION

A GUIDE TO SANITATION AIDS

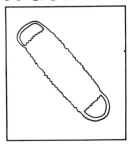

SANITARY NAPKIN
(makes a good hammock for mice)

BELT FOR NAPKIN
(available in soppy pink/white, but you can spray-paint them yourself)

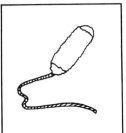

TAMPON
(put it in glass of water and watch it expand to 8 times its size. Fancy that in your vagina?!)

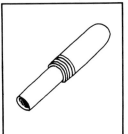

TAMPON INSERTER
(can be used as toy telescope for kiddies, by enterprising and creative mothers)

DOCK LEAF
(It will do if you're camping)

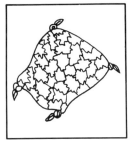

BATIK HANKY
(used by some African women)

SPONGE
(you can buy these on holiday in Greece. V. economical because they double up for the shower!)

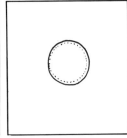

DUTCH CAP
(I'm not sure about this one, but apparently some women use this)

BARBED WIRE
WRONG! (not absorbent enough)

HOW FEMALE TERRORISTS WHO I ADMIRE (like Astrid Proll) MANAGE TO CONCEAL PROTECTIVE WEAPONS AT DISCOS (so you can really shoot from the hip!!)

1

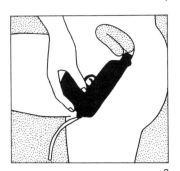

3

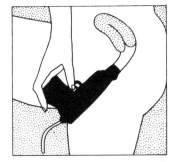

2

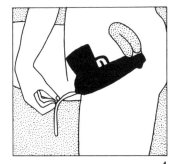

4

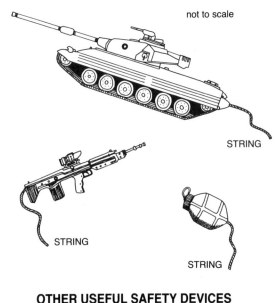

not to scale

STRING

STRING

STRING

OTHER USEFUL SAFETY DEVICES

SELF-EXAMINATION HOME KIT

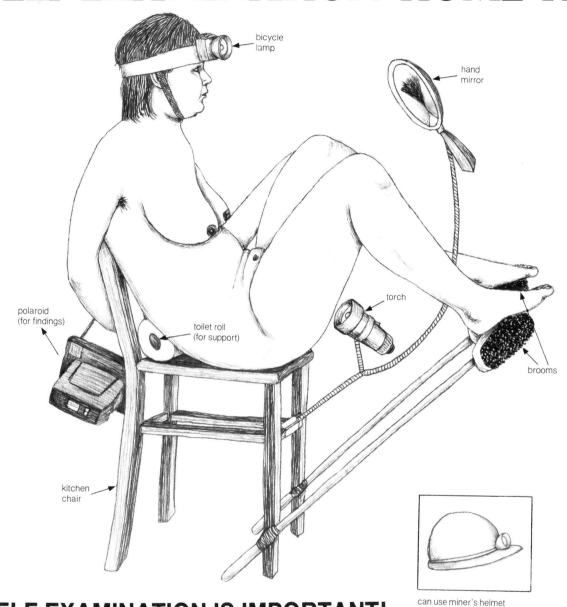

bicycle lamp

hand mirror

polaroid (for findings)

toilet roll (for support)

torch

brooms

kitchen chair

can use miner's helmet
(I've got one left over from picketing)

SELF EXAMINATION IS IMPORTANT!
IT CAN SAVE YOUR LIFE

A dentist's chair is ideal but if not easily available you too can make this simple, easy-to-lubricate, no-nonsense formica examination chair with only two egg-boxes, three squeegie bottles, some sticky-back plastic, a mirror and a bulb. Easily assembled – will clip on to any chair, e.g. aeroplane, train seat, hairdresser's chair, park bench, church pew etc. ('Do Your Own Pap Smear' spatula optional extra.)

Send large SAE to A Ripley and I will send you this 'Friendly Fanny Finder' by return of post.

Also, for expert analysis, send polaroids of your findings to above address. Discretion assured.

GYNAECOLOGICAL AWARENESS

Lecture
Tuesday 6:30pm

A guide round your toilet parts (on £5 a day)

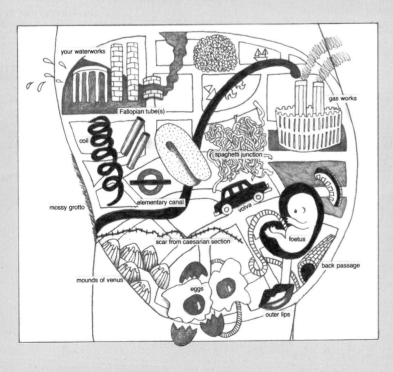

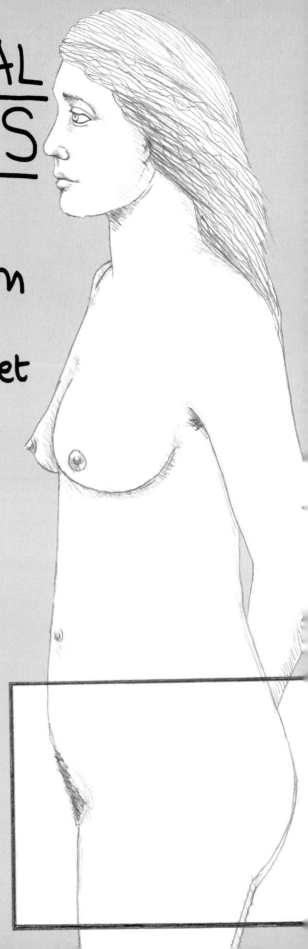

Shelley's Map of the World

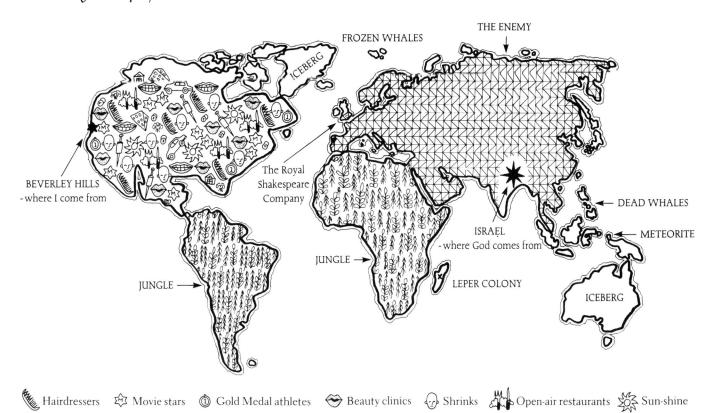

FROZEN WHALES

THE ENEMY

ICEBERG

BEVERLEY HILLS
- where I come from

The Royal
Shakespeare
Company

DEAD WHALES

METEORITE

ISRAEL
- where God comes from

JUNGLE

JUNGLE

LEPER COLONY

ICEBERG

Hairdressers	Movie stars	① Gold Medal athletes	Beauty clinics
Shrinks	Open-air restaurants	Sun-shine	
Qualified doctors	Good dentists	Available taxis	⑥ Money
Air conditioning	Delis	Country clubs	

Amanda's Map of the World

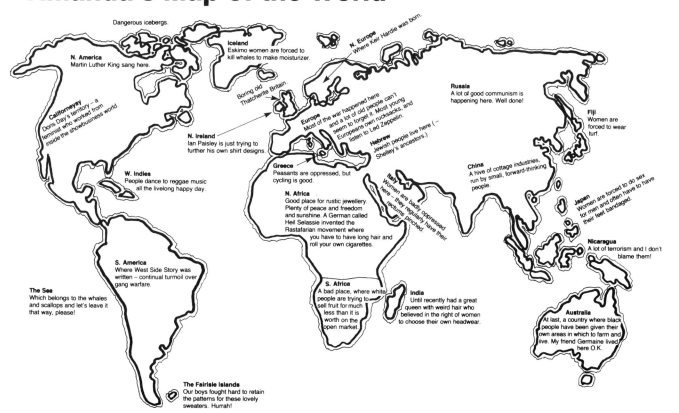

Dangerous icebergs.

N. America
Martin Luther King sang here.

Iceland
Eskimo women are forced to
kill whales to make moisturizer.

N. Europe
Where Keir Hardie was born.

Russia
A lot of good communism is
happening here. Well done!

Fiji
Women are
forced to wear
turf.

Californeysay – a
Doris Day's territory –
feminist who worked from
inside the showbusiness world.

Boring old
Thatcherite Britain.

Europe
Most of the war happened here
and a lot of old people can't
seem to forget it. Most young
Europeans own rucksacks, and
listen to Led Zeppelin.

Hebrew
Jewish people live here (–
Shelley's ancestors.)

China
A hive of cottage industries,
run by small, forward-thinking
people.

Japan
Women are forced to do sex
for men and often have to have
their feet bandaged.

N. Ireland
Ian Paisley is just trying to
further his own shirt designs.

W. Indies
People dance to reggae music
all the livelong happy day.

Greece
Peasants are oppressed, but
cycling is good.

Italy
Women are badly oppressed
here – they regularly have their
rectums pinched.

N. Africa
Good place for rustic jewellery.
Plenty of peace and freedom
and sunshine. A German called
Heil Selassie invented the
Rastafarian movement where
you have to have long hair and
roll your own cigarettes.

Nicaragua
A lot of terrorism and I don't
blame them!

S. America
Where West Side Story was
written – continual turmoil over
gang warfare.

The Sea
Which belongs to the whales
and scallops and let's leave it
that way, please!

S. Africa
A bad place, where white
people are trying to
sell fruit for much
less than it is
worth on the
open market.

India
Until recently had a great
queen with weird hair who
believed in the right of women
to choose their own headwear.

Australia
At last, a country where black
people have been given their
own areas in which to farm and
live. My friend Germaine lived
here O.K.

The Fairisle Islands
Our boys fought hard to retain
the patterns for these lovely
sweaters. Hurrah!

Jennifer's Diary

monday ~~good mor~~ ~~once~~ ~~upon~~ ~~Hello~~ Woke up on sofa. Took off nose clip. (Amanda puts it on to stop me snoring)

folded my blanket as usual. skipped! said "Good morning" to ponies, Grey Blue Black and orange.

They slept on my shelf. Sometimes they sleep on the sofa arm but are inclined to fall off and BREAK and SMASH!

Amanda says it's the vibrations from the snoring but Shelley says it's more likely that they commit suicide.

Sometimes they just fall off when I'm skipping.

SKIP SKIP SKIP

Found a stick insect in the kitchen put it in a jar with some bread. covered it with cling-film.

Must get a bigger bra!! Have to make one most probably.

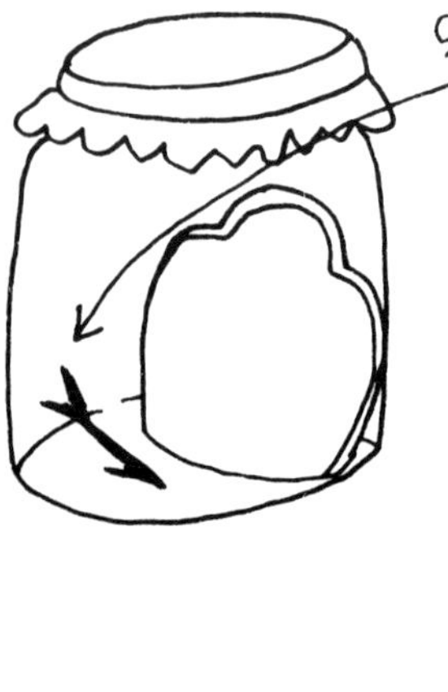

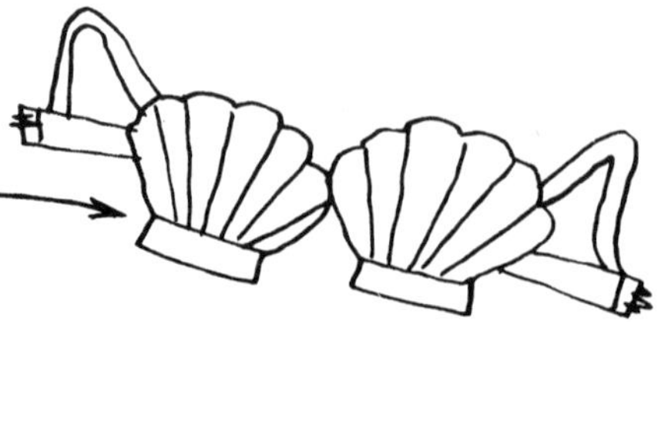

tuesday

me
amanda

Woke up on sofa, took off nose clip. SKIPPED! Then folded the blanket, put it in my corner. Put on wellington boots and rubber gloves. Did cleaning. I hate cleaning Amanda's room.

HATE HATE HATE !!

Candice has an ~~it~~ interesting part of the room. (Amanda says I'm not to go there though till rent o kill have been) She has some very clever posters of men and women sitting on each other to make up letters. I tried to do it with shells.

Shelleys room is best to clean she has a lot of dreamy photographs all over her wall. All of her! and some very expensive make-up. I touched some of the make up today and made up a story about her photograph.

Her ~~money~~ mother rang so I chatted to her mainly about money and make-up. She wants me to keep an eye on Shelley.

Stick insect still pretending to be a stick. I wont look at it so much its probably frightened.

I HAVE GOT A BAD RED LINE
UNDER MY BOSSOMS WHERE
MY BRA CUTS IN ON ME!

red line

wednesday AH OH! FORGOT ABOUT IT!

thursday woke up. Took off nose clip Skipped folded blanket.
Amanda said the stick insect was just an old twig infact and threw it in the bin with the bread which had gone mouldy. So it's just a bit of rubbish now.

DIDN'T CRY!

AMANDA IS JUST LIKE A PIECE OF HORRIBLE BROCCOLI!

Had to go to Marks and Spencers to buy some pants Spent nearly an hour finding the pants counter. NO SIGN! Only had bikini knickers. Tried them on in the shop but couldn't walk in them.

BIKINI KNICKERS

Tried to make up fuzzy-felt story before writing this but it wasn't very good.
Fuzzy-felt pets are :—

Dog ↗   Cat ↗   Bird ↘   pony (my favourite)   rabbit ↗

SHELLEY DUPONT'S GUIDE TO
OVEREATING
══I'M EATING AS FAST AS I CAN══

PIGGING-OUT

Just heard that Pia (the Bimbo) Isadora nabbed that film part you should have had?

Just noticed that all four wheels on your BMW have been clamped?

Or just discovered your flat-mate has been using your fifty-pound-a-bottle-eye-wrinkle-repair creme as cooking oil?

It's times like these you either hit the open blade or tear open that fridge door and ram till you're blue in the face.

After ten bloated years of taking choice number two (the Pig-out) Shelley Dupont can give you some hot tips on how to binge with a capital 'B'.

SHELLEY DUPONT'S RECIPE FOR MAJOR PIG-OUT

1. Use right hand if right-handed, or left if left-handed and open fridge door.

2. Bend from waist and undo buttons.

3. Thrust head toward foodal area.

4. Rip open oral cavity to full capacity and gnash teeth together. (Repeat this movement throughout)

5. Start, using mouth opening and shutting movements, from top left of fridge to right, left to right. As if reading a book with your gums. Slowly but surely moving downward from desserts in freezer across diary

products, slashing through left-overs, with a quick flick of the tongue to concessions on fridge door shelf (mayonnaise, ketchup, sweet and sour sauce) back to middle shelf for potato salads and slaw ending up on your knees for fruits and vegetables (optional).

9. Stand and allow stomach to assume new position: somewhere around the eighth month of pregnancy is usually standard.

10. Feeling of well-being and nausea should be so great you have forgotten original reason for pig-out.

6. Remember to spit out cellophane and foil as they could clog and cut down on full stomach capacity.

7. When circuit is completed, release legs and fall backwards. (Falling forwards with new load may lead to crushing of skull).

8. To get off floor whip-lash head forward and grab kitchen furniture for support. If this method fails phone fire department.

Standard shape
après pig-out ▶

HOW TO KNOW IF YOU'RE A TRUE PIG-OUTIST

Ask yourself these questions:

1. Do you use sex as a substitute for food?

2. You find yourself douching with an avocado dip?

3. On a dinner date, do you put food stains on your shoes to match your clothes?

4. After gorging on a rack of ribs, do you find some of your fingers missing?

5. Is orgasm only possible with the right chocolate chip cookie?

6. Do you carry a colostomy bag with you, so when you've filled up your own stomach you can plug in an extension?

7. Does your daily waist measurement read like 'From here to Eternity'?

THE WALKING PIG-OUT

Some pig-outters are also outdoor lovers (even gluttons like trees) so for them I recommend the 'Walking Pig-Out'.

The map below is only to guide you in planning a walking pig-out of your own.

Choose a street packed with edibles then just open your mouth and run.

Note – Before leaving home carry about 3–4 Mars Bars, or a stash of Rolos in case you encounter a 'closed' sign at a food source. (SEE – COLD TURKEY)

COLD TURKEY How to recognize a cold turkey (strangulation from foodstuffs) hour by hour:

Hour One of food deprivation – Stomach starts to sound like London Philharmonic.

Hour Two of food deprivation – Empty garbage bag in search of edible morsels.

Hour Three of food deprivation – Empty garbage bag in search of inedible morsels.

Hour Four of food deprivation – Start licking other people's lips.

Hour Five – Start marinating yourself in soy sauce.

Hour Six – Start playing zither on your ribs.

Hour Seven – Attempt to have sex with the bread box.

Hour Eight – Start to watch Dallas re-runs without the television.

Hour Nine – Áttempt suicide in the hope that they serve cheese balls in heaven.

RECOMMENDED ATTIRE FOR PIG-OUT

Leotard: make sure it's as stretchable as your stomach. (If it isn't, you may implode. Place 4–5 basketballs in it before use.)

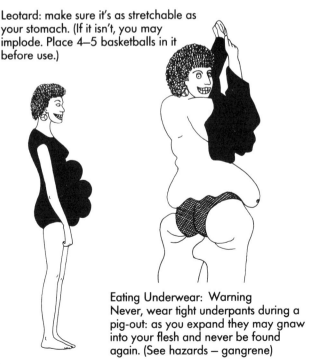

Eating Underwear: Warning Never, wear tight underpants during a pig-out: as you expand they may gnaw into your flesh and never be found again. (See hazards – gangrene)

And remember the Pig-Outer's motto: More!

"IF GLORIA STEINHAM CAN DO IT, SO CAN I"

In January 1963, Gloria Steinham answered an ad in an American newspaper, inviting attractive, personable young girls to become Playboy Bunnies and earn $300 per week. She undertook the assignment, armed with a large diary where she logged everything that happened to her, and then sold the story to a leading feminist magazine. It was an incisive report of overt sexism.

In July 1985, Amanda Ripley answered a similar ad in an English newspaper and went along to the Playboy Club in Mayfair for an audition, armed with a large notebook and a 'Women Do It With Their Vaginas' badge secretly hidden under her lapel. When she arrived, the panel of directors, all eight of them, simultaneously threw their heads back as one person and roared with hysterical laughter in her face.

Amid their cries of 'Why is God so cruel?' and 'Who sent the Roly-Poly-o-gram?', she was duly ushered out onto the street. Undaunted, she went round to the back and enlisted as a kitchen help, still determined to complete her assignment.

Here follows the report:

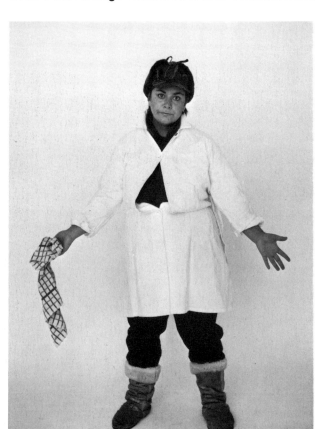

The first thing I noticed when I entered the kitchen was that I was the only woman there (besides a few unimportant washers and cooks etc.) . . . so I knew immediately that I was in for some serious oppression. And right enough, straight away, I was asked by the chef to 'put on an overall' . . . yes, well, I knew where he was coming from. It was so blatantly obvious. First of all, there's the idea of covering my whole body with a symbolically white garment (marriage, bondage, virgins etc.). Secondly, it was too small, so the buttons gaped open in sexually inviting and seductive way.

I managed to take a self portrait as proof with my hidden Kodak brownie, which I secreted between my thighs. It was a bit sticky but it worked and here's the picture:

Frightening, eh? Yes, I thought so too.

Anyway, I then went over to the sink and pretended to carry out the menial chores allocated to me by the fascist chef (who I later discovered, just as I had suspected, was called . . . Kevin). Underneath, I was frothing with inner turmoil just waiting, like a poised feline cat, to pounce on my first opportunity to expose this wicked den of sexist corruption.

I was lucky: it came, in less than five minutes, in the shape of Veronica, the 'Bunny Mother' who was

visiting the kitchen, she said, for 'a cuppa' (I expect she had really come to shoot up on some hard drugs so that she could force herself to go on living in this hell hole).

A wave of pity came over me and I quickly bundled her into the deep freeze room, whereupon I knocked her unconscious (I had to, for her own good. I knew she'd thank me later) (shame about the teeth).

Wow, suddenly it was all really relevant, I was liberating my first bunny. I knew Gloria would have been so proud of me. I stripped the Bunny Mother of her costume and ears and squeezed myself into that ridiculously non-expanding bondage costume the management think is so sexy. I then hopped into the club and quickly onto a roulette table to give my speech to my fellow captive bunnies.

Everyone was looking at me, so I started, 'Friends, Women, Rabbits, give me those ears and in so doing, escape from bunniedom forever!! I can help you all!!' The next thing I knew I was in a police cell, charged with disturbance of the peace and intent to incite myxomatosis . . . Phew! What a way to reclaim the night.

Next week, read my exciting true-life account of my prison sentence, entitled: 'The truth about being banged up'

Continued from p33

. . . Roger. Boy, did I meet Roger!!!

He was outside the gym one day, just sitting in his blue G.T. Capri . . . I had to face facts, I was in love with him immediately. My heart was thudding suffocatingly against my ribs, my palms were damp with hot sweat, but in that moment, I recognized a strange, new, different, varied emotion surging through my body – excitement, with a capital 'E'. Roger was different . . . he was old. About 72 or so, but I found the elasticky skin, arthritis and wispy grey hair a turn on. How would it feel against my soft tomboy belly? I climbed in beside him straight away and we drove to a secluded lane . . .

Continued p58

SOME GROTESQUE HABITS
OF THE ENGLISH
AND FACTS ABOUT ENGLAND

 WARNING Do not attempt to find a decent burger after 2.00 in the morning. Abort mission . . . it does not exist.

 WARNING They have not yet discovered the shower. They just fill up a tub and swim around in their own dirt. They *do* use rubber tubing resembling enema equipment.

 WARNING Never, never use a double-decker bus. Full marks for cute idea, but try coming down the spiral stairs when bus is in motion without having to go into traction for the next nine months.

WARNING Be prepared for the horror of seeing unlimited amounts of bodily hair found on females. To

my knowledge, no razor has seen the underarms of any woman in Great Britain.

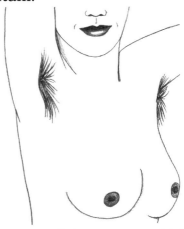

WARNING In winter, which is all year round, if you crave heat . . . forget it. Their only heating source is a piece of plastic in the shape of coal lit up by flickering orange lights. This idea is based on the same principle that if you show someone a photo of food, they'll feel full.

 WARNING Never go in a fish 'n' chip shop unless you like the taste of grease and last week's headlines. A chip is not a french fry as we know it, it's a stick of grease.

 WARNING Never go into a public toilet and expect to find toilet paper . . . bring your own. Also if by some miracle there is some – these people use wax paper which just moves your drips from one area to another.

WARNING If you see a corgi dog, curtsey. The queen has blessed them or something. (They look like Lassie but with no legs.)

WARNING The surgeon general has warned that pay phones may seriously damage your health. Do not, I repeat, do not use a pay phone if you have a heart condition or are prone to ulcers. You stand more chance of winning the jackpot in Vegas than getting through to anyone. There are no winners with Telecom. Plus that cross-beamed glass coffin they call a phone booth is also used as a public urinal (Must be another quaint old English custom to pee and dial all at once).

WARNING At a bus stop you will see this formation: a person faces another person's back and someone else faces his back and someone else faces his back, etc. . . . these people are what they call 'Queuing'. Do not use the American 'claw-your-way-to-the-front-method' or they will turn vicious. Find the last vacant back in the 'Queue' and face it.

WARNING Do not hit the ceiling when English people suddenly speak to you in baby-talk. These words are seriously used in conversation which is slightly pathetic when coming from the mouths of adults.

English Words –

Telly	Wally
Woolie	Sweetie
Wellie	Nappie
Willie	

I beat them at their own game by babifying my own words:

The airporty	Do you accept a
hospitalie	credit cardie?
Prime Ministerie	Bowelie
	face liftie

WARNING Your television screen really does go blank around midnight . . . you haven't gone blind.

WARNING Don't hold your breath waiting for plumbers, mailmen, car-breakdownmen or maids: you will die waiting. These people are actually very, very wealthy and run mega-corporations: they don't want your money, beg though you may for them to make an appearance.

WARNING In shops, banks and restaurants it is *not* your imagination – people really are moving in slow motion.

WARNING Don't be alarmed if you are hit by a car or involved in some disaster and an English person offers you a 'nice cup of tea'. It's their pathetic way of coping with any crisis.

WARNING Policemen are useless – they are unarmed and (I'm not kidding) sometimes on horseback (so they can just trot after muggers). Their sole purpose is to pose for tourists and provide a place (their hats) for pigeons to land.

This early warning pamphlet was provided to you courtesy of Shelley Dupont who has been coping in England for over 5 months and hopes that the knowledge gained out of the horrors of her experience here may help make your stay a little more tolerable and hygienic.

ME AND MY HATS

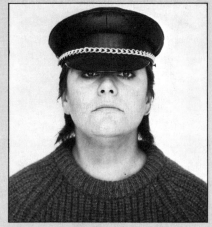

The 'casual about-town' hat

The 'so what's going on in Cairo these days' hat

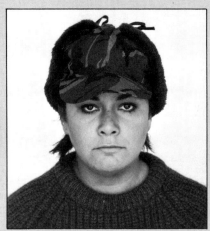

The 'don't give me any trouble otherwise you'll find a 2CV in your bottom' hat

The 'stripped pine in the country, long walks with labrador and plenty of real ale' hat

The 'yes, it's true, I've been to Yellowstone Park' hat

The 'my mother made me wear it to a wedding once' hat

The 'territorial army wouldn't have me so I bought my own' hat

The 'all-American I don't want to be seen by anyone at this David Cassidy concert' hat

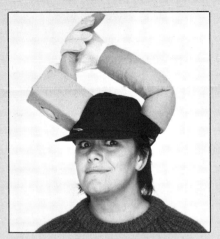

The 'whack and zane' hat

The 'friendly comrade' hat

The 'I know it looks stupid, but you'll be sorry when the frosts come' hat

The 'if you're as creative as me, anything in your wardrobe can be a hat' hat

The '*that* special date' hat

I AM NOT A CRIPPLE

Heartening and uplifting words by Candice Valentine

I HAVE NEVER BEEN ABLE TO GIVE IN, THERE IS A FIGHTER IN ME THAT SAYS 'CANDY DON'T LET GO', AND 'BY THE WAY, CRIPPLE IS NOT A WORD WE LIKE TO USE ANYWAY'.

I hope that the few words people may read here will give hope and faith to millions who like me, 'suffer'. I am not writing this for any personal glorification, publicity or a huge sum of money, but simply as an exorcism, a guide for others and a small sum of money to cover my expenses and medications.

Ever since I can remember, ever since I was just a teeny weeny little girl I have been a little 'sufferer'. I used to always be apart from my little kiddy classmates at school, because I knew I couldn't join in and play with them in their rough and tumble games. My teacher would say to me as I stood staring enviously out of the classroom window at the groups of children playing games, 'What's the matter with you now, Miss Valentine, too sick to play games again?' Of course I was, although I don't think she ever really believed or knew just how sick I was, and how I yearned to be out there with the others on those cold, cold winter mornings, scrabbling about in the mud. It was one of the things I missed.

There were two great towers of strength that I could lean on heavily when I was growing up. They were, my darling mum, and my nan. My darling mum would say to me 'Candy, my darling, I don't know how you endure so much', and 'What have I done to deserve you?' When my mum could take it no longer I would be sent to my nan's to suffer there.

I found great relief when growing up in being able to speak out about my illnesses. I didn't want people to be embarrassed when talking to me, afraid they might say something indelicate and hurt my feelings. I made people talk about illnesses, it made me feel better to go into graphic detail about them: I wasn't embarrassed so why should they be? I remember once I was taking school assembly and I was in the middle of describing my peristalsis problem and how I have never been able to have a proper osmosis when the Headmistress got up and with a pained expression said 'I'm sorry Candice, I don't think the school can take much more'.

So I said 'Don't worry about me Headmistress, the one thought that keeps me going is that I know that no matter how much I am suffering I'm lucky. Somewhere out there, there is someone who is even sicker than I am.' The

Headmistress said she didn't think that was possible, but I have lived by those words and it is that kind of thinking that has helped me get by and become the person I am today.

As an adult 'sufferer' (not cripple) I try to live as normal a life as possible. There is no point to just sitting at home moping, it is better to be out and about and giving as much pleasure and relief to others as possible. Some people say to me: 'You're not sick at all Candice, I don't believe it'.

It doesn't take long to convince them when I've put my mind to it. There will always be that 'doubting Thomas', that one 'thorn in your side' and they are not worth bothering with and wasting your energy on. Even if you dropped down in front of them and had an epileptic fit they wouldn't believe you, and I know, I've tried it.

Don't ever let people get on top of you unless you want them to, always be prepared to fight back, that is my motto.

I hope these words and the sharing of my experience will have helped someone somewhere and brought non-sufferers a little insight into the tragic world of the 'sufferer'.

Take care, lotsa care, Ciao!!

'DRUGGIE' WORDS

On Tuesday evenings, I host my own Drugs Victim Phone-in Help Line, and as you can probably imagine, I have to handle some pretty heavy cases. Last week, a young girl tried to inject a marijuana joint up her nose, and I can tell you, there was a lot of blood and gooey green stuff to deal with when I eventually got it out with a red-hot knitting needle. I'm just glad I was there to help.

Anyway, when people phone in with their problems, the most important thing is to understand what they're trying to say, so I have my *Glossary* near me at all times, so as to understand any references to drugs. I have compiled it myself after many years of helping others, being 'with the kids' and basically, having my finger on the pulse of what's happening in the youth culture of today.

A USEFUL GLOSSARY OF 'DRUGGIE' WORDS

ACID It really burns your fingers, I can tell you! Very dangerous.

BUSTED Being endowed with large breasts, useful for balancing a googly pipe when you're in bed.

COKE Mix this with four junior aspirin, and it makes you feel

quite tingly. Don't leave your teeth or any old pennies in it overnight, though.

DROP ACID Very dangerous ... if the test tube smashes, you could burn a nasty hole in the futon.

A FIX Jimmy Saville does it for children a lot (especially on TV). When, oh when can we stop this evil dealer?

GRASS Very common. Catch it fresh in bucket at back of lawn mower and smoke it. (Avoid dog doos.) I personally find it a bit smelly, but a lot of my poetry group like it ... and I think people should do what they want to, so long as noone gets hurt or raided by the police.

HASH Make it with corned beef and gravy. Some people get high on it, but my mother has been making it for years which just goes to show how modern she is.

L.S.D. Pounds, shillings and pence. Most old hippies are mentally retarded that they still use this old money for their drugs transactions. Quaint, but stupid.

PURPLE HEART A medal given to Vietnamese veterans. I think the idea is that it can be melted down and taken anally.

SMACK Do this to drug users at times of crisis, they'll thank you for it later. (The heavy, two-handed thwack about the head is a good technique: I practise on Jennifer.)

SHIT Some people smoke it – YEUCH! I say, put the grass back on the lawn and the shit back in the toilet.

HEROINE A girl to admire for having the balls, (sorry 'clit') to keep away from drugs. Right?!!!

September 15, 1985

Dear Mommy

I hardly have the strength to lift this pen with which I write, because daddy's pathetic allowance of $5,000.00 a month doesn't cover my basic survival needs i.e. facial, massage, pedicures, tints prunes and pluck. Mother I haven't had a full bikini wax in over three weeks and now have enough of a growth to make myself a kilt. I am addressed by perfect strangers as "Bush woman". I have of course been offered charity. Bob Geldorf even suggested having a pop concert to aid me but I told Bob, no, if my father chooses to skimp on supporting his only daughter and stand by watching her turn into a dog, let him; While my mother, his accomplice by default, refuses to tear a check out of his checkbook and send it to her needy child. A gesture she does at least six times a day for herself. I'd also like to mention my psychoanalysis with Dr Berenson has ground to a halt, since I can't afford to call Beverly Hills for my hourly sessions anymore. So I'm sitting here in London just brooding about how you deprived me in childhood by not buying me a mercedes coup when everyone of my friends had one. Dr Berenson always says to me no wonder I'm neurotic. Enough about me, how are you? Good. Sorry to hear Aunt Zelda's face-lift failed, but I told her if she had her eye-lids removed whe wouldn't look any younger, just more surprized. So tell her to not blame anyone but herself, when she blinks, she tears off her face. I <u>warned</u> her that just because Dr Lintberg removed Linda Evan's neighbor's corns doesn't mean he's a qualified cosmetic surgeon. Remember what he did to Mimi's nose? She asked for a ski-jump shape and the next thing she know is she's face-to-face with her own nostrils. She sneezed once and almost blinded herself. Anyway back to me again and my financial situation for a small point. If it doesn't improve soon and I'm talking tomorrow, I will be forced to tell daddy about your Mexican gardener Pepito and how he's been employed on an abundant salary for the last ten years from 9 - 5 daily. I mean how many times can a man mow the same strip of lawn over and over? And about the time I caught you squatting in your bedroom over a portable stove making tacos for Pepito's hacienda wearing nothing but a sombrero. I will also be sending copies of my Pepito report to every member of your "Beverly Hills - Nix the Spicks" volunteer group.

All my best
Your loving daughter

Shelley Dupont

Shelley Dupont

P.S. Check if Uncle Ruban is dead yet? If so, he owes me a lot of cash. (I read the will) thanks.

September 17, 1985

Dear Daddy,

What a coincidence, my funds have almost run dry and I'm writing to you. Some news first. Yes, they're still interested in me for the Royal Shakespeare Company, but Trev (Nunn) keeps telling me he has to get rid of Ian McKellen before I can join 'cause he doesn't want two brunettes in the company. Fingers crossed he chokes on a chicken bone! A few days ago I was invited to audition for a company called 7:84. I gave them my "highlights from Dynasty" piece ... you know where I play everyone and keep switching wigs. They were speechless when I finished, so just to cover the lull I asked them why they named the company after a bunch of numbers? They told me the numbers meant 7% of the population own 84% of the world's wealth. Well, I said, lucky thing they found me, 'cause with only 7% there aren't many of us around and wasn't that the beauty of capitalism? They got really hostile and suddenly I realised I was surrounded by communists. I left, fast. Really daddy, they think money should be evenly distributed. Well then, I ask, how can you tell who's rich?

Anyway back to the lack of funds situation. There is a slight problem with the allowance you sent me ... it isn't enough. Here is a run-down of my expenses in a typical week, so you can make the adjustments.

The week of July 29 to August 5.

Seven breakfasts in bed served by Jennifer .... £15.00 for food.
She gets no tip.

A leg and bikini wax by Candice .... £ 8.00 no tip

At-home body massage by Sven .... £75.00 The man is a
genius with his thumbs

Seven lunches at well-known restaurants to
meet influential people who can help my career .... £245.00 I tip big to
sit near the famous

I do alot of improvisational work with waxworks at Madame Tussauds.
Last week I slapped Henry the 8th for not giving me a divorce and
got fined for knocking his nose off £300.00

BMW repairs £548.00

FROM THE DESK OF
Shelley Dupont

(One of those punk people with green spikes strolled in front of the car. I thought it was a 'go' signal and they had to scoop him out of my heating vents. Don't worry, I'm suing him.)

Weekly phone bill to my shrink in Beverly Hills £360.00

(Dr Berenson has an answering machine that takes messages up to one hour. It's fabulous, I've left him about fourteen hours of Primal scream.)

Singing Telegrams saying "I'm in town" to Trevor Nunn, Lawrence Olivier, Vanessa Redgrave, and Andrew Rice Webber £45.00

Plus miscellaneous necessities: Tints, cellulite wraps, vitamin shots, gifts and flowers to stars, self-promotional billboards on motor-ways, in-depth interviews with myself in major magazines, pamphlets of resume and distribution over all of London and surrounding regions, Goodyear zephyrs with my name on them, and rental of Albert Hall for one-woman Shakespearian week-end with Shelley Dupont entitled "Shakes. with Shel. The Complete Works" (Bring a duvet and food) £3,876,00

So daddy, as you can see, my monthly allowance of £5,000.00 just doesn't cover, and if the cash situation isn't improved on, I will tell mommy about what you do with all her missing girdles.

Much love as always ...

Your daughter

Shelley Dupont

Shelley Dupont.

P.S. Is Uncle Ruban still alive? If not, he promised he'd leave me something ... check the will, Thanks...

THE ART OF 'THE MEETING'

How not to welcome people

I've been to a lot of meetings in my time, so believe me, I know the difference between a good one and a bad one! I am continually amazed by the amount of people who don't know how to conduct one properly. Didn't they do 'debating' at school? At present, I am 'chairing'* (and that doesn't simply mean sitting on a chair, ha, ha, thank you Jennifer) roughly eight meetings per week in my own home. I also 'attend'* meetings at the homes of my 'colleagues'* as well. I am actually invited to these a lot, so I definitely do know a lot about it. For example . . .

Here are the examples of 'good gatherings', 'mellow meetings', 'delicious debates', 'sensitive soirees', 'awesome airings' . . . as you can see already, there are 'multifarious'* species of meeting one can have . . .

1. Ordinary house meeting with other members of household. (Boring but necessary)
2. Larger house meeting including landlady and dog. (provide biscuits and choc. drops)
3. Meeting with a group, i.e. fellow members of 'Sisters in Trouble'. (I am the president of this organization)
4. Poetry reading. People come and enjoy me reading my latest works. (On the first Monday of every month with an 'e' in it, including May, which was originally spelt 'Mae'. I think Mr Wordsworth will support me on that issue!)
5. Action support group victim aid committee. (I am head leader of the world for this group. A lot of people have become victims since I joined. My motto – 'Everyone is a victim, I can show you what of')

6. Other meetings at which I am a useful person may include local community issues, e.g. Gay People against dogs (we have a lot of both of these in Chelsea) or women against make-up and Young People for Money, etc.

THINGS TO PREPARE BEFORE MEETING COMMENCES

1. Put note up on notice-board to forewarn other members of household, after all, that's only fair and democratic. (In my flat, a very good idea is to put the clocks forward that a certain person might be tempted

to go out and not stay in to be a total embarrassment. You can lose a lot of street cred if people find out you're living with a bunny girl. Also, buy one ticket for 'Bambi' and present it to Jennifer for that particular evening, it's a cert.

Get my friend Roz who is a dresser at the Prince Charles Theatre to ring up Shelley and ask if she'd like to meet Bonny Langford in person backstage. So far, I have done this six times and each time Roz puts the costume on, pretends to be Bonny, signs Shelley's autograph book and promises to get her into musicals.

2. Make book of tickets, putting a secret non-transferable mark on every single one so that noone can gate-crash. (There are quite a lot of culturally-starved people in Chelsea who are desperate.) Get 'friends' to sell tickets. If you can't sell them, give to people in super-market, preferably those in 'health food' dept. please!!

3. Think seriously about cater-ing, i.e., e.g. and therefore, should you provide squash and biscuits or is it more of a home-made bramble hock and crêpes sort of evening? Only you can decide. (Word of advice, only serve food *after* meeting – I usually find there are a lot less people then and it isn't wrong to have small flags in food

explaining the price of each item, after all we all have to live and clingfilm doesn't grow on trees!

4. Re-arrange furniture. This is very important, I always make sure I have the stockiest and highest stool so that I can be fully seen and heard. After all, sometimes we get over seven people to the victims' evenings.

If I need a lectern for my notes, I borrow one from our local church. (Not that I'm into God or anything, but Colin, our 'vic.', is really progressive and preaches that Jesus was Bisexual, so he must be alright. He's also encouraging

a lot of the young boys from the primary school to come to his 'Jesus touches us everyday, so let's touch each other work-shops'. Nice bloke.)

5. Prepare your speech into a mirror, practising a lot of stri-dent facial and hand gestures to add impetus. (See photo) This is a good technique ... many world leaders (one in particular who had thousands of followers) have used it in the past very successfully.

6. Get someone to take the minutes, preferably someone who can write with joined-up writing, unlike my numbskull secretary. (See photo) These

notes don't have to be too pre-cise; so long as what I say is carefully taken down and later typed up neatly and sent out as a memo, that's OK.

7. Voting. Basically, try to vote on as many things as possible. Last week I wanted to check that everyone was concentrat-ing, so I took a vote on how many people were in the room at the time. The resulting numbers varied enormously: it was very interesting. Also, a useful tip is to have a vote on who everyone thinks is the nicest, most leader-quality-type-person in the room. I always win this and that in

My secretary

itself shows that voting is a fair and important method.

8. The final word of advice ... crowds tend to mumble away aimlessly amongst themselves unless they're given some sense of direction, so a good thing is to shout very loudly through a meg phone (see photo) so that everyone knows you are the most important person. Otherwise, if I'm not heard – how on earth are we ever going to change the world!

(* means see glossary)

---

* GLOSSARY (Jennifer tried to write it in joined-up writing, so she couldn't under-stand it when she read it back – sorry)

PET FOOD

1. SPAGHETTI HOOP FLOATERS
(recommended for all types of fish)

Get a tin of delicious spaghetti hoops and open them. They smell gorgeous don't they? Have a good long sniff and imagine how hungry your fish might be getting . . .

Then tip them into the aquarium and look how lovely they look floating down to the bottom. Don't forget only tip in half a tin, the other half is for you – so you can enjoy them too. Don't save all the lovely tomato sauce for yourself make sure Sammy the goldfish gets a good lump of it too. Sometimes the fish enjoy it so much they start imitating the spaghetti hoops and float to the surface on their backs. This is very funny and makes me laugh.

2. MIXED GRILL
(recommended for rabbits)

Jennifer tests every recipe so it is safe for your pet

You can grill anything as long as it is mixed.

Take some eggs and mix them with some spaghetti letters and some sausages, and some sardines, and some parsley for flavouring, and vitamins.

Then serve with a tomato garnish.

These recipes are all tried and tested by Jennifer herself.

3. PLASTICINE BAKE (recommended for 'My Pony' Only)

Take a selection of different coloured plasticines. Make the red bits into carrot shapes, the blue bits into sausage shapes, the green bits into cabbages, the brown bits into balls and the yellow bits into flat bits.

Then put them all together in a small flower pot and put them into the oven for 1 hour. (Remember – do not switch oven on – this is just pretend)

Remove from oven and serve with a garnish of parsley for vitamins and flavour.

'My Pony' likes to eat out of a shallow dish. As it is pretend leave the bits in front of him or her for a couple of minutes then remove them bit by bit so it looks like he or she is eating. BUT DON'T BE TEMPTED TO POP THEM INTO YOUR OWN MOUTH.

WARNING
THIS IS NOT SAFE TO EAT YOURSELF. I WAS VERY SILLY TO TRY AND THE DOCTOR SAID IT WAS THE MOST STUPID BIT OF BEHAVIOUR HE HAD EVER SEEN FROM A GROWN ADULT HUMAN BEING AND IF I WENT ON DOING SO HE COULD EASILY HAVE ME PUT IN A SAFE PLACE. SO EVEN THOUGH I HAVE BEEN TEMPTED I HAVE NOT TOUCHED A PLASTICINE BAKE NIBBLE SINCE.

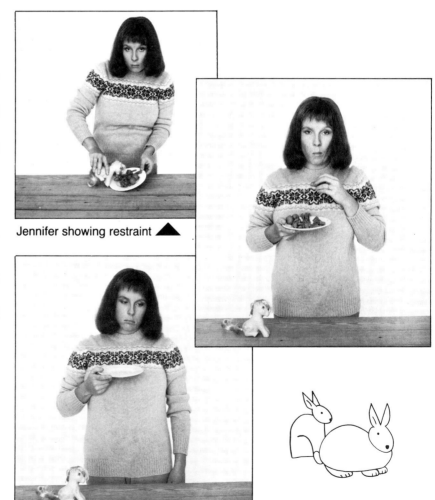

Jennifer showing restraint ▲

ALTERNATIVE
Nursery Rhymes

FOR JENNIFER
By Amanda Ripley

Mary, Mary quite contrary,
How does your garden grow?
I'm surprised it can grow at all in Inner London,
With all the used durex all in a row.

Round and round the garden,
Like a dirty old man,
One step, two step,
Knee him in the danglies if you can.

Baa Baa Black Sheep,
Do you feel oppressed?
Let's rip your skin off,
And use it for a vest.
One for the Prime Minister,
One for a page three girl,
And one for all the other racist,
    sexist people in the world.

Jack and Gill went up the hill
To try their relationship out.
Jack fell down
And broke his futon
And Gill was a lesbian anyway.

There was an old woman who lived in a shoe,
She had so many children, she didn't know what to do,
The social worker visited and took them all away,
If she bothered to use modern contraceptives,
    they would have been able to stay.

THE MISSING LINK

By Amanda Ripley

Below, I put to you a very simple and obvious solution to an evolutionary mystery that scientists have been baffled over for years. Why they haven't spotted the answer completely escapes me – maybe it's because they weren't at school with her for seven years . . .

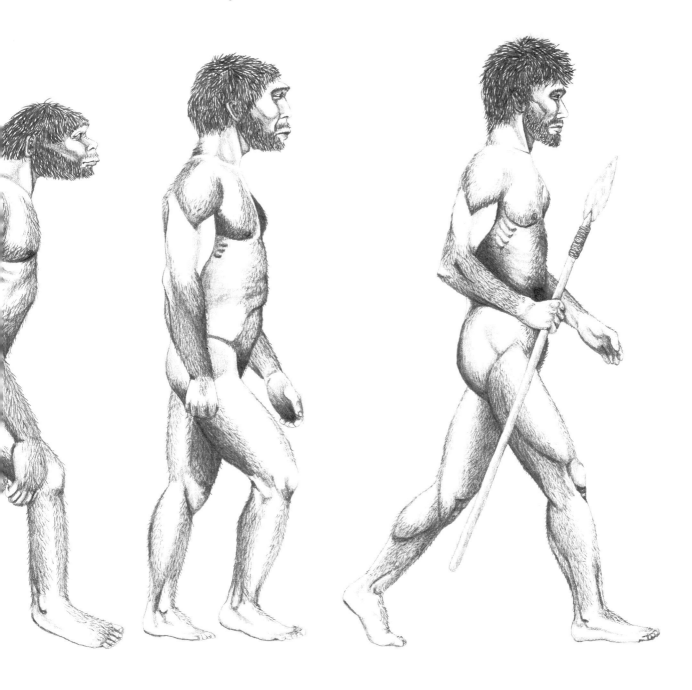

NATURE

DICTIONARY DEFINITION – Nature n.l. Thing's essential qualities.

Well, this may well be so, but, it's not what I think it is that's for sure. 'Nature' is what you do at school and what you go for walks in the woods for: it is things to collect and kill and study and look at and cut up and press, e.g: insects, spiders, fish, birds, beetles, trees and earth. Nature is all around us especially in the country which is mostly 'nature'. It is living things and dead things, e.g: leaves, that form a whole big thing called 'Mother nature' which is what makes everything work properly and mustn't be interfered with under any circumstances.

In big towns and cities like London, where I live now, it is harder to come by good nature and you have to walk further and look harder to find it. Not everything you step on in London will you want to pin in your scrapbook, e.g: chewing gum, fish and chips and dog poo.

MAKING UP YOUR OWN NATURE COLLECTION

This is when you collect bits of nature and stick them in cotton wool in drawers or nail them to a board. Insects are good to collect because you can find them easily and catch them easily by treading on them or putting a jar over them and waiting for them to die. Butterflies are harder and often you end up with just a wing or a leg or an antenna. A method not to use which is very silly and mustn't be tried is throwing a jar at them and hoping you will catch it in midair. *WARNING.* DO NOT THROW JARS AT BUTTERFLIES. THEY SMASH AND BREAK AND COULD HAVE SOMEONE'S EYE OUT. I TRIED IT AND IT DID NOT WORK.

•By Jennifer

Some things I managed to collect in London:-

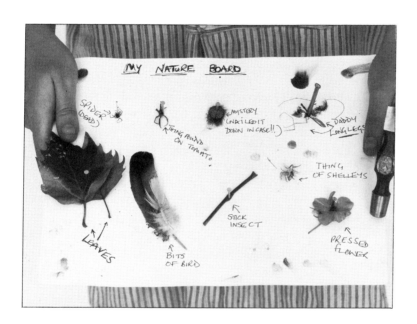

MY NATURE BOARD

SPIDER (DEAD)

←MYSTERY (NAILED IT DOWN IN CASE!!)

→DADDY LONGLEGS

←THING FOUND ON TOMATO.

THING OF SHELLEYS

←LEAVES

↑ BITS OF BIRD

↑ STICK INSECT

↑ PRESSED FLOWER

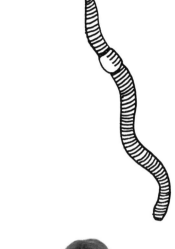

Nails, glue, or sellotape are the best methods of sticking down insects and things. If they are not quite dead when it comes to sticking them down it is best to use sellotape as it is less messy than nails.

The Conservation of Nature is very important, without it where would we all be? What better way of conserving nature than a 'nature board' like mine? (See above). So you see I am doing my bit and hope that in years to come, future generations of nature enthusiasts can look at my board and learn something.

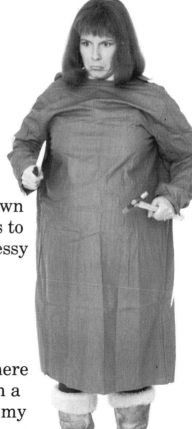

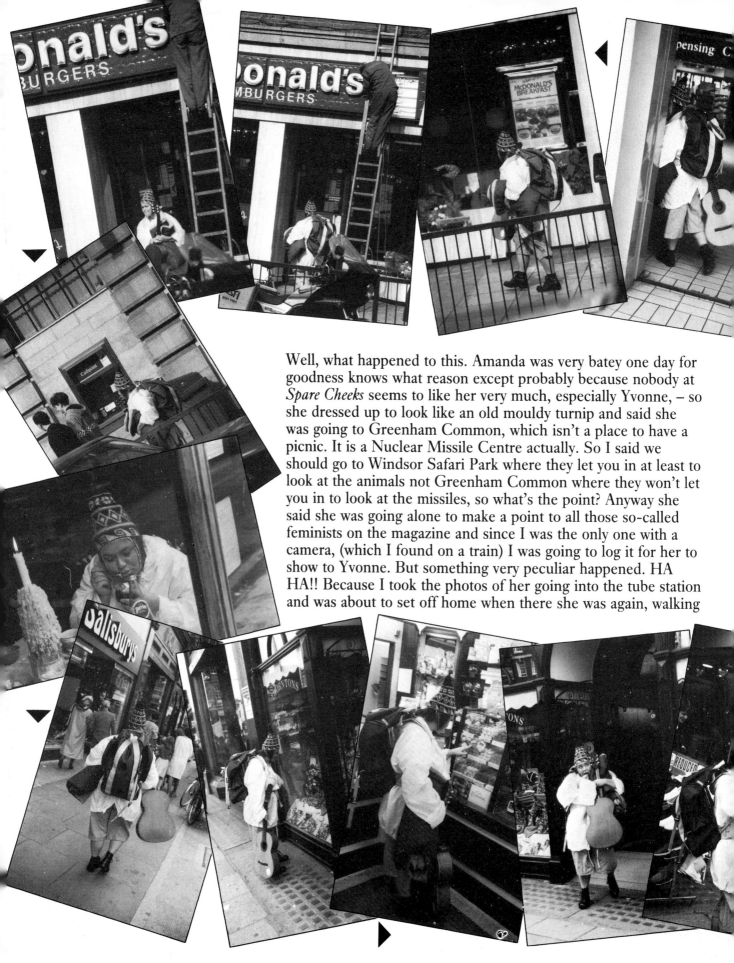

Well, what happened to this. Amanda was very batey one day for goodness knows what reason except probably because nobody at *Spare Cheeks* seems to like her very much, especially Yvonne, – so she dressed up to look like an old mouldy turnip and said she was going to Greenham Common, which isn't a place to have a picnic. It is a Nuclear Missile Centre actually. So I said we should go to Windsor Safari Park where they let you in at least to look at the animals not Greenham Common where they won't let you in to look at the missiles, so what's the point? Anyway she said she was going alone to make a point to all those so-called feminists on the magazine and since I was the only one with a camera, (which I found on a train) I was going to log it for her to show to Yvonne. But something very peculiar happened. HA HA!! Because I took the photos of her going into the tube station and was about to set off home when there she was again, walking

along looking like a Hobbit (which is one of my most favourite books) and going to have a hamburger in the hamburger place which is very peculiar seeing how as she had ten breakfasts before she left. Then out she comes, walking, walking, walking and I though 'oh no she's going to walk to Greenham Common which is probably over a mile away as the crow flies', when she goes into another place for some more supplies. I'm surprised they served her because she looked so odd, but I expect they were frightened by her or she threatened them with death or 'Baby Jesus' which always works on me.

Then out again and more walking, walking, walking and into another shop and then out and then, oh dear! She just went completely mad. Which is what happens when you eat too quickly and have too much chocolate my mother says. Now nobody has a camera.

JENNIFER ▲ LOGS AMANDA'S TRIP TO GREENHAM COMMON

LADY CARLTON...
A LIFE IN THE DAY
–ROOM OF MY OWN

6.00 P.M. One fluttering sun-speckled lid is seduced open by the beckoning, hot, oily torso of the day. I toss off the delicately pungent sheets, still drenched in my nocturnal odours. I attempt to open my other lid, but it stubbornly remains in its crusted igloo. I rise from my dormitory bower, my arms outstretched to embrace my long lost lover, the sun; when suddenly the daily round of horrendous machine-gun fire, buzzing chainsaws and crescendoes of a thousand tortured screams begin in the purgatorial abbattoir of my skull . . . My knees crack onto the solid floor, and I blindly crawl, flailing pendulously from side to side, in desperate search of that porcelain font, commonly recognized as 'the loo'. Finally there, I relieve myself in one great volcanic torrent of bubbling hot poisonous gases and fluids in homage to last evening's entertainments. I sponge myself down; my ablutions complete, I am ready for my day.

My meagre breakfast consists of plenty of roughage, nuts in their shells, followed by two thimblefuls of Retsina. I float to my desk, and metaphorically punch in my work-card at the factory of literature, my typewriter. Just at that precious moment, I hear the familiar yappings and playful growlings of my darling Josephine, begging me for a scampish romp . . . Thirty-five years old, and still a puppy!! 'Mummy, mummy,' she cries 'get down on all fours and play with me' . . . Inevitably, I surrender, and there follow many joyful hours of sniffing each other and playing 'Fetch the Bottle'. At long, exhaus-ted last, languorously lolling on the shag pile, we toast each other's happiness with a healthy shot of gin each. I implore Josephine to cease, for I must needs return to my novel . . .

I wait patiently for the spirit of inspiration to fill my bowels with the creative muse, and if it doesn't show up after six hours, I hit the meths. Instantly, my fingers are a frenzy of action upon the typewriter keys. My head reels with visions of pink-crinolined princesses having their maidenheads torn viciously asunder by rampant sea-captains; husky, bearded highwaymen savagely biting into the swanlike necks of the serving wenches on the candlelit gondolas . . . white chargers, naked gardeners, whipped flanks . . . Complete novels leap, lemming-like, from my keyboard. Such classics as 'Oh, My Slippery Heart' and 'The Jolly Protruding Highwayman'. Bravo! Bravo!

I awake from my prolific fit with a shudder and slump forward, exhausted, sweating and frothing. I am washed up in a sea of paper, I clasp one in my hand and there, in front of my eyes, I read . . . 'HMZPHXGDROLKING'. How clever, I have been typing in tongues!!

I lurch to my kitchen for a celebratory hit of morphine, and the rest of the evening is usually spent with visitations from famous historical figures . . .

'Mr Livingstone, I presume?'

Lady Carlton, novelist and lady of pleasure ▶

Continued from p41

. . . I was all hands and tongues immediately. I was surprised to find that Roger had a colostomy bag but with a little unplugging and a lot of care, he was a great lover, and we did things with a gearstick that I had never dreamed of. We thrashed around from the glove compartment to the big end, wildly. Who would have thought a man of 72 could be so bendy??!

Afterwards, when we lay back in the seats, sweating and heaving with lustness, he told me the terrible, dreadful awful truth . . . he

was Lance's father!! Oh God, how could he have deceived me like that?

I felt bad and went home for a long luxurious foamy bath to cleanse myself of his sticky love-juices and accidental excretions. But it was too late; I discovered I was pregnant.

Roger had a wife who was in a wheelchair with no legs and had been barren for years and she longed for a baby, but couldn't have one.

Oh God, I married Mr Muscles, and spent my nights with his father and now I'm pregnant with another woman's child . . !!

THE END

MY GUY

I hate parties, give me a good meeting any day.

I hope no one talks to me, then I can go early.

You chewing a brick or talking about me?

The slow back-swing.

Hey, look at this one – she's got a face like a bag of chisels.

Who's this suspicious-looking character?

Looks like some sort of vicious oppressor. Thank goodness I don't want any men in my life, no siree.

Mind you, he's above average in the good-looking stakes, maybe, just this once, it wouldn't hurt if he came back to my place and we played 'hide the sausage', oh, if only . . .

First contact.

Let me cherish your head in my hands.

Actually, parties can be quite good fun.

PRINCESS SHELLEY

Perched in the Wind

MY MEMOIRS
By Shelley Dupont

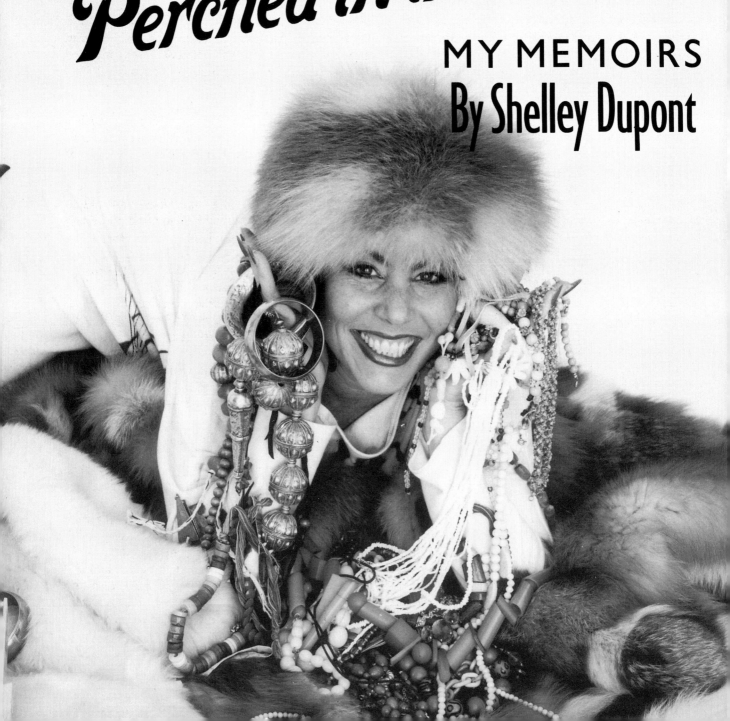

CHAPTER ONE
The Early Years

In 1841 my grandparents, Ivor and Latka Dūpønzkchkvich$kä (my family name before it got axed down to Dupont) were borscht-pickers in Wvskinski, Poland. There is absolutely nothing interesting about them so, jumping ahead . . .

In 1958ish I was born, a girl, overweight (the bane of my life), and adorable. The delivery took longer than it should have because my mother refused to uncross her legs and leave the gin rummy game she was winning. She just held her ground, throwing back the pain killers, mopping up her own waters while shouting, 'deal me in you bastards, I'm on a roll.' This is the same woman who contemplated a tummy tuck in her seventh month of pregnancy and she has never forgiven me to this day for the stretch marks. Her doctor suggested not to breast feed me as they were too full of artificial ingredients – the silicone would probably kill me, so I learnt to drink Tab at an early age. I had my primal scream experience at four when I discovered all the other kids in my neighbourhood had motorized tricycles and I had to pedal mine. That's when I started to see a shrink who said I should never forgive my parents for that slip-up. I never have.

I was an only child and was determined to keep it that way . . . no way was I going to split my salary. I sent my parents a memo saying if I ever saw a flicker of a brother or sister entering my home, they would go straight into the microwave. Then things took a turn for the worse, I was starting to lose my original gorgeousness. My teeth began to stick out so far that they were in another time zone . . . they were about an hour ahead of my face, and my father started to use me as a bottle-opener. Plus I realized to my horror that my head had stopped growing, but my nose hadn't, so I broke it myself with the piano lid. Luckily surgery stepped in and I regained my classical looks.

At six I was sent off to be with children similar to myself at the 'Beverly Hills Day-Camp for Affluent Children'. Every morning we had to line up in order of our father's income – from the most to the least. The girls in the 'least' end were cut off from ice cream, so we were really forced to appreciate the power of the dollar. We were also encouraged to start our own entrepreneurial projects: I had the other girls invest in my 'canoeing-for-dollars' venture, sank mid-way and claimed bankruptcy . . . I made a killing.

We went on assorted field trips. One day we visited poor people in their natural environment. We all had to have shots before we went and then we actually rode on a public bus. (We put paper towels on the seats so we wouldn't catch rickets or anything). We then went into a single-storey house and met a no-maid, one-TV family. I had a photo taken of me next to the mother who does the cooking and cleaning herself (I'm not kidding). I gave her some food I brought along in a care package.

Then we visited a second-hand clothes shop. Finger-down-the-throat time, I wouldn't blow my nose in the stuff. (I was glad we had the shots.) At the end of that day, as my dad's Cadillac whisked me down our tree-lined driveway, past the pools and Japanese Bonsai gardens and I blew a spit-ball at Pepito, our gardener, I was glad I had gone out that day and seen how other people lived. And suddenly I had a blinding moment of clarity . . . a moment when you feel you comprehend the universal truth that embraces all reality. It was at that moment I learned the most important lesson I would probably ever learn for the rest of my life. I learned that I have absolutely nothing in common with those people and that my role was to be rich and theirs was to be poor. I wept at my own inspiration and sped on . . .

ALTERNATIVE AMANDA'S BEAUTY TIPS

3 EYELASHES
Never touch something called 'mascara' – it is made out of whale testicles and gives you cancer immediately.

4 UPPER LIP
A rich dark fuzzy down is nothing to be ashamed of – I'm not!

Important to maintain a smiling, happy, broad countenance so that when you are really angry, people know the difference. Bright eyes, good even teeth and a wet nose are essential. Start with top of face:

1 FOREHEAD
Don't worry about lines, they help to make your face 'characterful' and 'quirky'.

2 EYELIDS
I've got a lot of what I call quantity in this area. Good for shade on hot days.

5 CHEEKS
Plenty of room for extra supplies of food you might need to store when winter comes.

8 MOUTH

The bigger, the better. There's much work to be done with this orifice.

6 EARS

God gave us two of these, for listening with, not for puncturing and hanging gross tin effigies from. By the way, did you know that ear wax makes great candles when our brothers in the mines are on strike.

11 CHIN

As many as possible, please! These chins enable you to develop dimples and keep certain strappy hats on.

9 TEETH AND GUMS

Always useful, so take good care and eat at least two raw steaks per week; use dried blood from these to make sausages.

Finally, the crowning glory:

7 NOSE

Congealed germs gather at the entrance with the aid of nostril hairs, so please do not tweezer these hairs unless you want bogeys in your brain (like Ronald Reagan).

Keep as short and manageable as possible. This also helps to avoid lice. I find hair a nuisance, you have to wash it *every* fortnight and it gets in your eyes and clogs up your hairbrush. Its only purpose is to encourage dandruff, so I'm having mine all cut off tomorrow. Well, soon, anyway.

10 TONGUE

As in 'you'll feel the rough edge of My' – mine is long wide and rough – exactly right for tactile reassurance of a special friend.

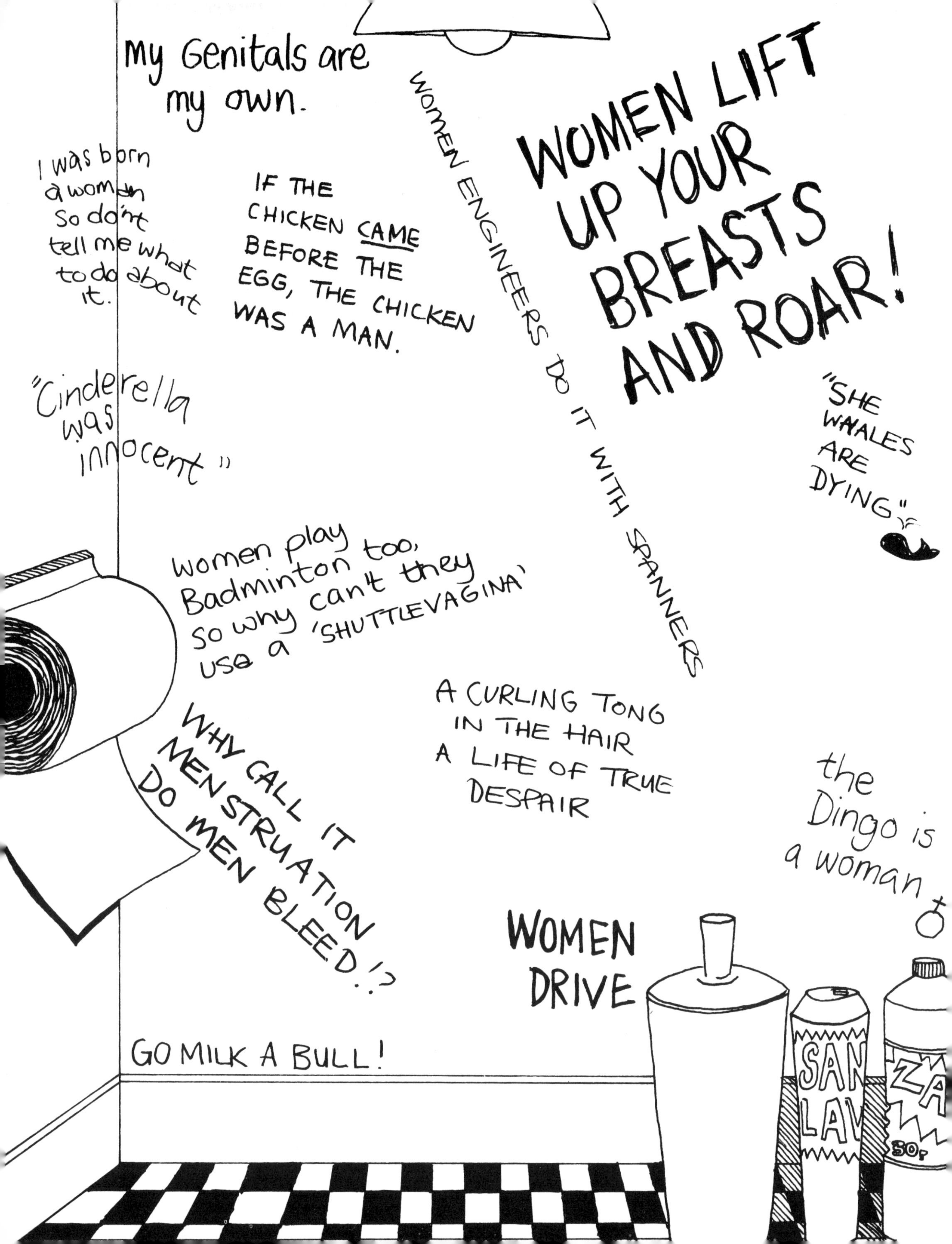

My Genitals are
my own.

I was born
a woman
so don't
tell me what
to do about
it.

IF THE
CHICKEN CAME
BEFORE THE
EGG, THE CHICKEN
WAS A MAN.

WOMEN ENGINEERS DO IT WITH SPANNERS

WOMEN LIFT
UP YOUR
BREASTS
AND ROAR!

"SHE
WHALES
ARE
DYING"

"Cinderella
was
innocent"

women play
Badminton too,
so why can't they
use a 'SHUTTLEVAGINA'

A CURLING TONG
IN THE HAIR
A LIFE OF TRUE
DESPAIR

the
Dingo is
a woman ♀

WHY CALL IT
MENSTRUATION
DO MEN BLEED!?

WOMEN
DRIVE

GO MILK A BULL!

SAN
LAV

ZA

80p

THE KANDY KWIZ

Are you a SURVIVOR?

Someone tells you the earrings you're wearing are theirs, do you . . ?

A. Apologize for stealing them and offer to buy them another pair?

B. Throw a moody, fling them back in their face saying they're not your taste anyway?

C. Explain about the resident poltergeist and other strange phenomena where things mysteriously appear on your body?

Your girlfriend has picked up the man you fancy, do you . . ?

A. Say he's a nice bit of stuff and that they look lovely together?

B. Terminate the friendship with a sprinkle of Ex-Lax in her babycham?

C. When she's in the loo, explain to him how happy you are that at last she's found a man who doesn't mind about her mastectomy. Push your own breasts into his face saying, 'They aren't the most important things in the world are they?"

You know you can't afford next month's rent, do you . . ?

A. Apologize profusely and promise to take a part-time job?

B. Take money temporarily from pockets of friends. After all you'll all laugh about it in a year's time?

C. Point the accusing finger the other way saying you don't know who anybody is, that you paid your rent last week to somebody, clutching your head and saying nothing's been the same since the concussion. Then ask pathetically what your own name is?

You're late for an important modelling assignment and leaving your parking spot you accidentally reverse over a pedestrian on a zebra crossing, do you . . ?

A. Give her the phone number of your insurance company and suggest she do you for all she can (offering to donate any organ required from your own body)?

B. Cradle her lacerated head in your arms, point at the dent in your bumper and scream was she ever taught the green cross code?!

C. Reverse over her again and drive off at high speed eliminating other potential witnesses en route?

You need a holiday, do you . . ?

A. Ring a respectable travel agent and book a package holiday?

B. Apply to become an air hostess, train exhaustively for five years and accumulate enough flying hours to earn one week's leave in the location of your choice?

C. Pack a vanity case, go to Heathrow and immediately report to lost property. Explain your handbag containing tickets, passport and money was stolen and you are going to your mother's funeral in Bahamas/Jamaica/Virgin Islands and cry until you take off?

Given a selection of fast money-making schemes, would you . . ?

A. Babysit?

B. Put white contacts in your eyes, paint a stick white and stand on street corners with a mug?

C. Get to know Bob Geldof's brother, offer your services in the Live Aid Charity offices opening the envelopes (and getting to meet famous personalities into the bargain)?

You're on your way to sunny Greece: suddenly the engine fails, the aeroplane nose dives, do you . . ?

A. Adopt appropriate crash position, make sure seat belt is fastened and table is stowed, and pray?

B. Slap air hostess and fight way to cockpit. Knock out pilot and take over controls in desperate rescue attempt?

C. Grab as many fat people as possible and wrap them around you to act as human cushion during impact. Single out the largest person and keep hold – you need to eat him/her later?

You get engaged to Amud and go for a fabulous weekend in Istanbul. It's all romance and roses, then you find you're not the only woman in his life, you're locked in his harem: do you . . ?

A. Accept the yashmak?

B. Not accept the yashmak?

C. Seduce guard number one into your cell, knock him over the head with a handy hookah, dress up in his clothes and exit from the building. Jump into laundry basket of passing camel who drops you off at Bedouin camp. Travel with them until you arrive at oasis where you meet snake charmer and become his dusky assistant. Travel to big city with him, and pack yourself in a crate of Turkish Delight and wait to be shipped home?

Answers to the Kandy Kwiz.

If you've answered A to the above, you are what is considered 'Nice'. Definitely not 'survivor' material. Start a crèche, take up crochet. Give up now: there's not much to look forward to.

If you've answered B to the above, you're almost there, but a real survivor gives the ulcers, not gets the ulcers.

If you've answered C to the above, congratulations: you're a true survivor, your skills have elevated you to the top of the heap. Welcome to the high life, babe.

Recommended reading for those who wish to improve their survival skills:

'Jet-setting on £5.00 a day'
'Gate-crashing with ease'
'The who's, where's and how muchness of Arab Princes'

A POEM ABOUT FREEDOM

(this poem is going into a whole book of my poems and is going
to be sold in aid of the many still suffering in the Greek islands;
where I spent two weeks widely travelling last year, both by boat and
bicycle, so I know about it)

A postcard sent to
Gloria Steinham
whilst on holiday.
(It was returned to
me, I don't think
she lives at the
address I've got anymore

Freedom, Freedom, Freedom,
  When will we speed 'em
          up?
Those liars who promised it?

Ha! Ha! Hee! Hee!

They must laugh in their tyrranical government offices,
"So they think we're giving them freedom, do they?"

This is freedom...
  No hospital treatment for our children
      with very sore veroukas,
  No decent wooden flooring
      on which to dance bazoukas, bazoukis?
  No reduction in the price of petrol,
      for our vans to deliver pitta bread,
  No newly-minted coins to put on the scarves
      us colourful peasant women wear around our heads.

Not sure this bit scans

AND taramasoulata, and humus?
  What of they? O, Government man ??????????

A. Ripley ♀ x

THE ENEMY

Jennifer, if you ever have the unfortunate luck of being in close proximity to one of these, (1) don't panic (2) follow the procedures I suggest, then you will be safe.

Thwack w/ cricket bat, makes great noise and is 100% effective.

Easily removed with razor/penknife.

A quick jab w/ fingers should help to sharpen that focus.

Can be ripped off in handfuls w/ great vocal effect, should shirt be unbuttoned.

Vulnerable area (full of lager and curry): head butt immediately and get out of the way quickly.

Underdeveloped and dangerous: clasp w/ tweezers and turn in clockwise motion.

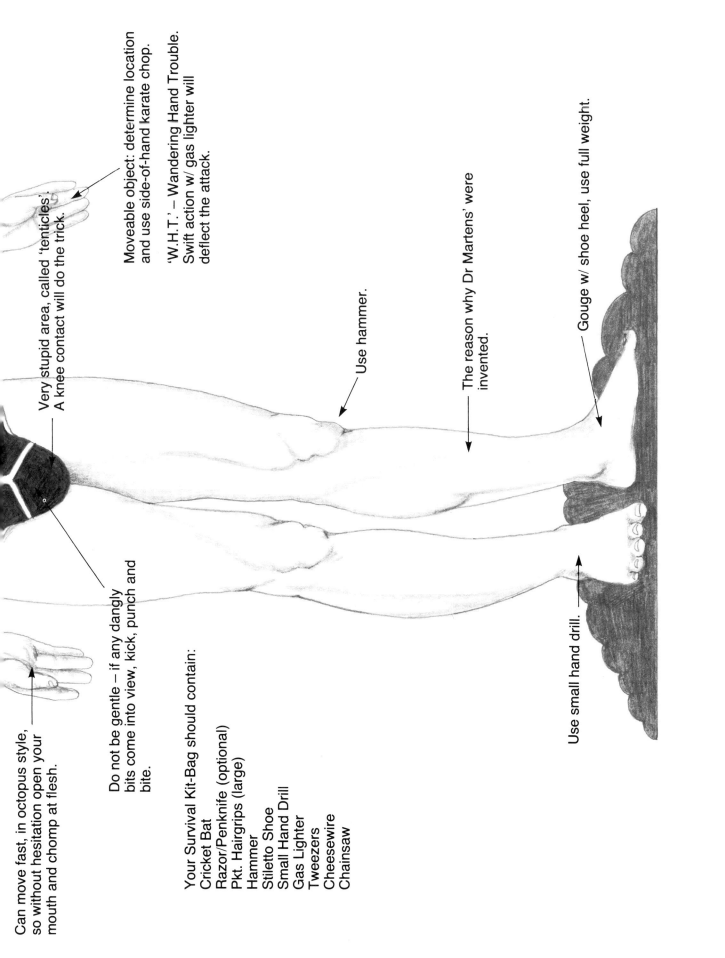

Can move fast, in octopus style, so without hesitation open your mouth and chomp at flesh.

Very stupid area, called 'tenticles'. A knee contact will do the trick.

Moveable object: determine location and use side-of-hand karate chop.

'W.H.T.' – Wandering Hand Trouble. Swift action w/ gas lighter will deflect the attack.

Use hammer.

The reason why Dr Martens' were invented.

Gouge w/ shoe heel, use full weight.

Do not be gentle – if any dangly bits come into view, kick, punch and bite.

Your Survival Kit-Bag should contain:
Cricket Bat
Razor/Penknife (optional)
Pkt. Hairgrips (large)
Hammer
Stiletto Shoe
Small Hand Drill
Gas Lighter
Tweezers
Cheesewire
Chainsaw

Use small hand drill.

FAMOUS PAINTINGS

I WISH I'D BEEN IN

By Jennifer Marsh

THE MONA LISA – Da Vinci

Why She gets a lot of attention which must be rather nice.

THE LAST SUPPER – ?

Why It must be nice to have a dinner party where so many people come, and they all like you and have fun and eat the food you make.

THE CHARGE OF THE LIGHT BRIGADE – Anon

Why I always wanted to be a vet and there is none in this painting, looking after the horses.

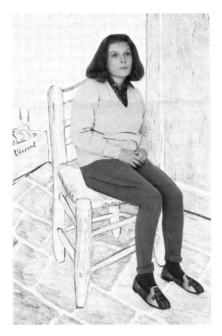

THE CHAIR – Van Gogh

Why It looks comfy. I think he probably meant to paint a person in it but must have been distracted. By his ear falling off maybe.

SLEEP – Salvador Dali

Why His paintings always make me laugh. This one especially reminds me of how I feel a lot of the time (like when Amanda is talking to me).

THE BIRTH OF VENUS – Botticelli

Why I like flowers and nature and especially big shells. It must be very strange being born out of a shell. It must be funny being a mussel.

INTIMATE POSITIONS ON BOEING 747

(1st Class – *do not attempt 2nd Class*)

1 'Excuse me, sir, I was just using the sink' position

2 Half in/ Half out position

3 Prepare to dock

4 The sudden turbulence
position

5 Fasten my seat-belt,
bitch

6 'Chicken, meat or fish,
sir?' position. My
favourite position

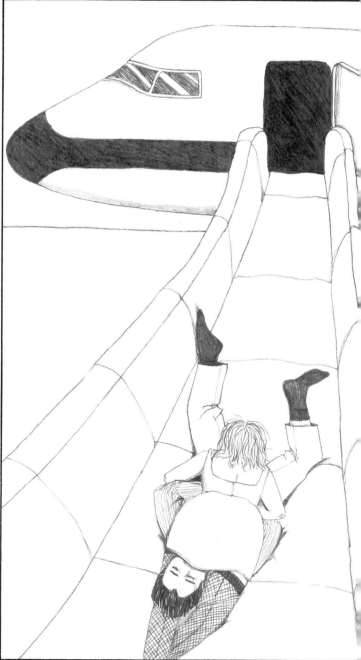

7 In case of crash-landing
no need to curtail your
pleasure

The Kandy Wig

You too can so easily look like the lovely Candice Valentine in all her multifarious feminine moods. Just one small crossed cheque or postal order, and all those hours of struggling with the tongs and heated curlers are things of the past.

These wigs bond with your own hair with the aid of only one squirt of magic Kandy wonder spray (only 7.99p extra) which has of course been scientifically researched in my Swiss laboratories.

Also, use the special Kandy Komb (4.00p), and the special Kandy Kurbies (3.00p)

STYLE A69   STYLE A53

STYLE B24   STYLE 42B

STYLE A92   STYLE A24

JENNIFER

JENNIFER

SHOP

AMANDA
RIPLEY
REPORTS